V&R

Religion, Theologie und Naturwissenschaft/ Religion, Theology, and Natural Science

Herausgegeben von
Willem B. Drees, Antje Jackelén,
Gebhard Löhr und Ted Peters

Band 20

Vandenhoeck & Ruprecht

Pascal Boyer

The Fracture Of An Illusion: Science And The Dissolution Of Religion

Frankfurt Templeton Lectures 2008

Edited by Michael G. Parker and
Thomas M. Schmidt
Afterword by Wolfgang Achtner and
Elisabeth Gräb-Schmidt

Vandenhoeck & Ruprecht

Bibliografische Information der Deutschen Nationalbibliothek

Die Deutsche Nationalbibliothek verzeichnet diese Publikation in der
Deutschen Nationalbibliografie; detaillierte bibliografische Daten sind
im Internet über http://dnb.d-nb.de abrufbar.

ISBN 978-3-525-56940-5

Umschlagabbildung: „Zitat", 1996, Acryl, Papier, Holz 100 x 100 cm © www.edeltraut-rath.de

Acknowledgments – and a cautionary note

This is an extensively modified version of lectures presented at the universities of Frankfurt and Gießen in May 2008, as part of the Templeton Research Lectures on science and religion. I am very grateful to Dr. Wolfgang Achtner and Dr. Elisabeth Gräb-Schmidt for organizing these lectures, and to Dr. Thomas M. Schmidt for publishing them in this series.

Dr. Achtner, Dr. Gräb-Schmidt and I also engaged in extensive discussion of the material presented during the lectures – and the revisions are largely due to their input, as I greatly benefited from their intuitions and criticisms. I hope the text does reflect some of the pleasure of these friendly exchanges, although these scholars are of course not responsible for any of my outrageous claims.

Being lectures, these were delivered in the form of sermons – that is, in this case, with greater emphasis on argument than evidence. I provide only minimal description of the studies, experimental and anthropological, that lead to the particular claims made here. I chose to take as my starting point what we know from the scientific study of religious thought – not how we came to know it – and explore some implications for such questions as: Can there be a free civil society with religions? Does it make sense to talk about religious experience? Do religions make people better? I encourage readers who find some of these statements odd or implausible (and the study of religion is replete with surprises) to have a look at the studies mentioned in the notes.

Contents

1. Is there such a thing as religion?

The point of this book is not to argue that religious ideas are creations of the mind. That point was conclusively argued more than two centuries ago by Kant and other *Aufklärung* scholars. We are all in debt to the Enlightenment – and conscious enough of that debt, that we need not restate what was so lucidly demonstrated at the time.

No, the point here is to carry on where these scholars left off – this time with the use of a better science – and show that the very existence of some thing called "religion" is largely an illusion. What I mean by "illusion" is actually very simple, but also rather counter-intuitive and therefore difficult to present in a succinct yet persuasive manner. Most people who live in modern societies think that there is such a thing as "religion", meaning a kind of existential and cognitive "package" that includes views about supernatural agency (gods), notions of morality, particular rituals and sometimes particular experiences, as well as membership in a particular community of believers. In all this, each element makes sense in relation to the others. Indeed, this is the way most major "religions" – Islam and Hinduism for instance – are presented to us and the way their institutional personnel, most scholars and most believers think about them. By considering, studying or adhering to a "religion" one is supposed to approach, study or adhere to that particular package: an integrated set of moral, metaphysical, social and experiential claims.

All that is largely an illusion. The package does not really exist as such. Notions of supernatural agents, of morality, of ethnic identity, of ritual requirements and other experience, all appear in human minds independently. They are sustained by faculties or mechanisms in the human mind that are quite independent of each other, and none of which evolved because it could sustain religious notions or behaviors. What would seem to be integrated wholes, the Shinto system or the Islamic world-view, are in fact collections of such fragments.

So why do religions, and by extension religion, appear to be such integrated wholes, such systems? That is largely a matter of stipulation. That the package is a package is not a fact but the wish expressed, or rather the slogan put forth with great animus by the members of many religious institutions – the priests, the ritual officers, the office-holders in religious institutions. There is no reason to take this postulate at face-value. Indeed, there is every reason to think that the notions of a religion (the Hindu religion, the Islamic religion) and of religion in general, are the main obstacles to the study of why and how people come to have what we generally call "religious" notions and norms, that is, why and how they find plausible the existence of non-physical agents, why they feel compelled to perform particular rituals, why they have particular moral norms, why they see themselves as members of particular communities. These phenomena cannot be understood unless we first accept that they do not stem from the same domain, they do not actually belong together, except in what amounts to the marketing ploys, as it were, of particular religious institutions.

The notion of "religion" as a package seems so plausible that even people who intensely dislike what they see as the supernatural fantasies, odd rituals or extravagant moral exigencies imposed by religious institutions, still assume that there is such a thing as religion – which they see as a nefarious set of thoughts and institutions, the influence of which has increased, is increasing and ought to be diminished. Framing the conflict as a struggle of reason or lucidity against the obscurity, indeed obscurantism, of a single enemy, "religion", simply perpetuates the illusion that there is a domain of religion – a single fortress for the militant rationalist to assault. That it is an illusion may explain why the best efforts in this epic struggle are often in vain.

Incidentally, the view presented here implies that there is no such thing as a conflict (or even debate) "between science and religion" – at least not in the way that confrontation is generally described. This is partly because natural science does not really *compete* with the statements of religious institutions about the natural world – scientific knowledge quite simply makes them entirely redundant.

It is also because "religion" in the religion-science debates is quite simply an imaginary object, a chimerical combination of widespread metaphysical beliefs, culturally acceptable moral norms, and the doctrines of religious institutions – but that amorphous mixture does not really exist, either as a set of mental phenomena in anyone's heads or as a social or cultural phenomenon.

Whether "religion" is a mere illusion or not is not an academic matter, given the social and political implications. One could hardly write about the topic and ignore the presence of many people bent on inflicting serious harm or death on others for what seems to be an extreme form of religious adherence. Is religion to blame? Framing the question in such terms ensures that we will reach no understanding of the phenomenon. Once we leave aside the "religion" label, there are many useful things we can learn about such violent extremism from the behavioral and biological sciences.

In a less dramatic form, a variety of political debates in some countries (the USA and countries in the Middle-East in particular) seems to focus on the putative role, if any, of "religion" in the public sphere or on the connections between "religion", civil society and the state. I will argue that such debates may become much less murky, and perhaps even rationally tractable, if we dispense with the notion that "religion" is one of the partners in the debate. There is no such thing. Belief in the existence of a social object that is "religion" is equivalent to belief in this or that form of supernatural agency. It is a stipulation produced by religious institutions, not a statement of observable fact.

There is something slightly Quixotic about insisting that something you *know* exists, something you talk about every day, just isn't what it seems, or doesn't in fact exist at all. So it is quite reassuring for me that this position – that the existence of a "religion" package in the mental and social life of humankind is largely a myth – is actually supported, if not explicitly endorsed, by much empirical research in the social and neural sciences. What we know in a naturalistic and scientific way rather than just intuit from everyday cognition about the way minds work and the way human societies are constituted suggests that there is no such thing as religion. How that changes our perspective on many issues, and of course most importantly, on the way humans acquire what we usually call "religious" concepts and norms, is the topic of this essay.

The Kant-Darwin Axis

The classical question in the scientific study of religious cognition was formulated by Immanuel Kant with (uncharacteristic) elegance and cogency more than two centuries ago, in the preface to his *Critique of Pure Reason:*

Human reason has this peculiar fate in one domain of its knowledge, that it is burdened by questions which, as they stem from the nature of reason itself, it unable to ignore, but which, as transcending all its powers, it is also unable to answer. This leads reasons to engage in ambiguity and inevitable contradictions.[1]

The answer, the reason for the obscurity and the contradictions, was just as clearly stated:

The ambiguity into which [reason] falls is not due to any fault of its own. It starts with principles which it has no option save to employ in the course of experience, and which experience at the same time justifies.[2]

The demonstration that followed was rather less straightforward, to put things mildly, but the main point remains in all its strength. The reason why there are

1 KANT: "Die menschliche Vernunft hat das besondere Schicksal in einer Gattung ihrer Erkenntnisse: daß sie durch Fragen belästigt wird, die sie nicht abweisen kann; denn sie sind ihr durch die Natur der Vernunft selbst aufgegeben, die sie aber auch nicht beantworten kann [...]. Dadurch aber stürzt sie sich in Dunkelheit und Widersprüche, aus welchen sie zwar abnehmen kann [...]". Kant, *Kritik der reinen Vernunft* [1781], A VIIf.
2 KANT: "In diese Verlegenheit gerät [die Vernunft] ohne ihre Schuld. Sie fängt von Grundsätzen an, deren Gebrauch im Laufe der Erfahrung unvermeidlich und zugleich durch diese hinreichend bewährt ist [...]". Kant, *Kritik der reinen Vernunft* [1781], A VII.

religious beliefs and behaviors is not to be found in metaphysics but in epistemology – or psychology, as we now call it – in the workings of the human mind. Beliefs in gods and spirits are not explained by the existence of gods and spirits, but by mental assumptions about agency. Beliefs about the origin of morality are not explained by moral codes and commandments, but by the way humans' minds represent moral judgments. Beliefs about the need to perform rituals are not explained by ceremonies and their symbolic exegesis, but by mental processes that govern our motivation for and representation of action.

We are now vastly more knowledgeable than Kant about the workings of the mind, as the domain of inquiry gradually shifted from philosophy to the natural sciences. What Kant and most philosophers until recently treated as a matter of pure reasoning – trying to figure out how minds work and why human beings attach such great importance to some peculiar ideas – has become a matter of experimenting, testing theories, establishing models and running more experiments. Like all scientific developments, this produced a jungle of models and results. It took some time for the dust to settle and for everyone to realize that we now know more than we ever did before. But we do – and we can better understand the appeal and implications of religious thoughts, among many other domains.

We are now also much better informed as to what is human about human beings, in the sense that we know much more about our own species than we used to. The main development here is that of evolutionary biology from Darwin onwards, and of molecular and evolutionary biology in the twentieth century. This has provided the background against which we can explain the appearance and persistence of behaviors, but also the mental capacities that support them. The fact that human minds entertain religious thoughts and feel compelled towards religious behavior is among the many aspects of human nature that make sense in the context of evolution by natural selection.

The Kant-Darwin axis is an apt conceptual foundation for the science of things religious i.e. for the explanation of religious thoughts and behaviors in terms of natural processes. As Kant demonstrated, religious thought is parasitic upon the normal use of human reason – but we know a lot more now than Kant did about what that normal use entails and how religious notions can become attractive, attention-grabbing and apparently compelling. As Darwin and Wallace originally suggested, behaviors and capacities of living things, including the mental capacities of human beings, result from the cumulative influence of millennia of selective pressure, as ways to increase the fitness of their bearers – but we now have much better knowledge of how the process actually occurs and how it builds minds with all their specific propensities.

Religions without doctrines

The focus on what we are familiar with – those highly doctrinal phenomena people call "world religions" – is the source of confused views about religion. For instance, it is in my experience exceedingly difficult to convince most people of simple facts that are familiar to any anthropologist: that most religious thought is not about the creation of the world, that it is rarely about God, that it is very seldom about the salvation of the soul. Most people in oral transmission cultures show little interest in the creation of the world or the origin of evil. They generally see no direct link between the behavior of a person during their lifetime and whatever happens to the "soul" or "spirit" – if there is such a notion – after death.

It is important to insist on these points, as it is very difficult to keep them in mind when discussing religious thought and behavior. Too often, such discussions take for granted that we all know what religion is – and this implicit notion happens to be a vague precipitate of all the familiar "world-religion" traditions. Also, religions of the non-world format are dismissed as archaic or unimportant, since most people these days live in contact with some form of organized religion. This however is not a terribly sound argument, as people in modern places have the same minds as those who live in traditional cultures with simple technology. Indeed, I will argue here that the actual religious thoughts of modern folk are much closer to traditional forms than we generally think. Membership in organized religions modifies people's spontaneous religious thoughts much more than is generally assumed.

Equally important and even more difficult to impress upon most people: most "religion" has no doctrine, no set catalog of beliefs that most members should adhere to, no overall and integrated statements about supernatural agents. Most religion is piecemeal, mostly implicit, often less than perfectly consistent and, most importantly, focused on concrete circumstances. People use their religious concepts to account for their uncle's death or their child's illness or their neighbor's good fortune, not to explain the persistence of evil or the existence of the universe. This puts a special gloss on Dr. Faust's famous lament:

I have now studied Philosophy,
And Jurisprudence, Medicine,
And even, alas! Theology, [...]
And here, a poor fool! With all my knowledge
I stand, no wiser than before.[3]

---

3 GOETHE: "Habe nun, ach! Philosophie,
   Juristerei und Medizin,
   Und leider auch Theologie
   Durchaus studiert mit heißem Bemühn.
   Da steh ich nun, ich armer Tor." *Faust* [1790], 3.

So that knowing theology, or being conversant with the scriptural traditions, does not, unfortunately, add much to our understanding of religious thought and behavior, because most human societies throughout history have managed to have religion without theology.

Most religious thought has no doctrine for any of the standard metaphysical questions, because it has no doctrine at all. If we understand by doctrine a minimally integrated set of coherent assumptions about supernatural agents, their powers, the justification for rituals, the ways some people can interact with gods and spirits, etc., it is quite clear that in most groups in the world one can find no such thing. This has in some quarters fuelled a long-lasting misunderstanding between scholars of religion and anthropologists. The former assumed that people outside organized religion must have some doctrine, only a rather esoteric one, or a mytho-poetic one, or an enacted one; the anthropologists tried hard to show that in most human groups coherent religious behavior is combined with vague, fragmentary, idiosyncratic and often less than perfectly coherent accounts of superhuman agency.

Moreover, as far as anthropological and cognitive evidence can guide us, the situation is quite similar in groups where there is some official religious doctrine. Again, this is one of those anthropological findings that some students of religion do not seem to register, or whose import they fail to see. In places where a doctrine is available, indeed where people are taught that doctrine, and themselves believe they hold the beliefs typical of the doctrine, there is large and converging evidence that their actual thoughts and intuitions diverge widely from the doctrine. People may well be taught and repeat that religious agents are transcendent, yet they see their gods as very close interlocutors; they are taught and repeat that gods are omniscient and in fact assume that the gods have cognitive limitations, like any human being. They are taught and repeat that a statue is just a symbol of the god, yet assume that the actual artefact is endowed with special powers.

No "religion" in most cultures

All this may explain another familiar anthropological finding. In most human cultures there is simply no word to designate a package that would include ideas about supernatural agents, moral imperatives, rituals and other prescribed behaviors, taboos, the building of a community around a common cult. There is no word – and missionaries from world religions often resorted to neologisms to designate what they were trying to impose in those places – and in general there is no concept either. For most people in such societies, there is simply no clear connection between the notion that dead people become invisible spirits, the notion that you should not kill your kin, and the idea that marrying your cousins is proscribed (or prescribed). Often, there is no connection at all between dead ancestors who protect you and forest spirits that may or may not be helpful. If you tell people that both notions belong to a single domain they find that puzzling. Ideas about forest-spirits are connected to other ideas about the forest. Ideas about ancestors are connected to other ideas about dead people and the family. But there is no "religion" umbrella concept that would put these two supernatural notions together.

Does that mean that in such places "there is no religion"? Some anthropologists are tempted to think that people's categories more or less define their world, so that people who have no concept of x have no x. So on this view, in places where there is no concept of religion, there is no religion. This inference however is question-begging, and assumes the very point it purports to demonstrate. It is obviously true that in some cases having a concept is necessary to create a reality. People who have no concept of cricket or parliamentary elections certainly have no games of cricket or parliamentary elections, because such social institutions only exist among people who have a roughly similar understanding of a specific set of concepts and norms. But it is equally obvious that in other cases concepts are unnecessary. Whether people have a notion of demography or economy or not, they all have demography and they all engage in economic transactions. When some anthropologists say that people without a concept of religion have no religion, they are assuming that religion is like cricket, rather than like demography. But this assumes precisely what we want to understand.

So is "religion" like the economy, something that you find in most societies although in many places people have no concepts to describe it? That position too is fraught with problems, because what people "have" outside organized religions is certainly not the same as what we are familiar with from religious institutions. I will also try to show that what the actual religious thoughts of most members of organized religions have little to do with what we commonly call "religion", and very little to do with what these religious institutions profess. So we should always keep in mind a clear distinction between completely different sets of phenomena:

Religious thoughts and behaviors – I will give a catalog of these in chapter 2. At this point we can just say that they consist in, among other things, notions of superhuman agents and agent-like artefacts, notions and norms about people's interactions with such agents, prescriptions about rituals in connection with these agents, etc. Such concepts, norms and behaviors seem to have been present in most human groups for as long as records are available, and as we will see, they have many features in common across times and places – which of course does not mean that they are universal or inevitable. You do not need to have a concept of what is and what is not "religious" to have religious concepts, just like you do not need to have a concept of economics to have economic transactions.

Religions – these are sets of norms and concepts offered by religious institutions (churches, sects, castes of priests and other such corporate groups) in the form of interlocking, integrated "packages" as described above. Before we get into any further description of these packages, note that religions in this sense have been absent from most human groups for most of human history. They are a recent development.

The terms defined above denote observable phenomena – people's thoughts and actions and norms. I will contend that we can perfectly well study these phenomena without the need for a third notion:

Religion – using this term is, I insist, tantamount to adopting a particular ideology, following which the packages described above are found, in some form or other, in all human groups – in other words, that the various religious thoughts and behaviors that we can observe in many places are instances of religions, particular manifestations of this natural kind of human experience. The following chapters should show that it is possible to make sense of religious thought and behavior without that notion.

Who invented religion?

Why is it the case that some human societies have that extra accretion of concepts and social relations centered on supernatural concepts? Why is there "organized religion" and indeed a notion of "religion"? The way this process is described by religious groups themselves is in terms of a myth of origin. The narrative says that a new doctrine appeared, that it gradually convinced more and more people, that the doctrine stemmed from a set of important texts or from a revelation, that proper transmission and maintenance of the doctrine and rites required an organized group of scholars or priests. So the tenets of doctrine came first and their social effects were among the many consequences of people's adherence to those articles of faith.

Obviously, such a narrative belongs to fairly-tales rather that serious scholarship. What the historical evidence says is both more complicated and more plausible. Complex polities originated in a few regions of the world, a few millennia ago and became states, small kingdoms, empires or city-states. Their economies and embryonic markets meant that many activities became the province of specialized groups, craftsmen in particular. These groups or guilds worked as cartels, often maintaining an exclusive grip on the delivery of particular goods or services. They organized training, often kept a *numerus clausus* of new practitioners, sometimes arranged uniform prices and often guaranteed a certain quality of service. This happened in most trades and crafts, for the intensification of agriculture meant that most people were too busy to practice these activities and that enough surplus was generated to feed specialists.

The provision of religious services is no exception to this trend. Together with guilds of merchants or blacksmiths or butchers there appeared groups of ritual officers and other specialists of the supernatural. They generally operated a monopoly, with an exclusive right to perform particular rites. They formed centralized organizations that maintained a strict control over new candidates. They tried to bind themselves as closely as possible with the sources of political power.

Before getting into the details of what these institutions were like, let me emphasize how this situation stands in stark contrast to what happened in human societies before or outside large states. Most of modern human history took place in small-scale communities that did not have any religious institutions. This was also the case of most human groups outside modern economic development until recently, and it is still the case in remote places outside the direct influence of modern states. In such places, there are generally no "priests" or scholarly specialists. What we find, on the other hand, are some people whose social position makes them closer than others to superhuman agency (lineage elders in ancestor-cults) but also people commonly held as "special" in that they have a particular talent for interaction with superhuman agents (this is the case of shamans, mediums, diviners for instance). Now these specialists generally do not elaborate a consistent or even an explicit doctrine of their own activities, but generally have a conceptual tool-box with appropriate recipes for various circumstances. They rarely see themselves or are seen as members of a category (*the* diviners or *the* shamans) and of course even less of a social institution. They are personally known to their customers. Indeed, most people think that the service offered by such a specialist is valuable because of inner, special qualities of that particular individual.

This personal-transaction market for religious services is what the newly constituted guilds of religious specialists disrupt wherever they appear. Religious guilds, being cartels of specialists, tend to unify the provision of services: that is, they try to promote the notion that, to some extent, the same service will be provided by any member of the guild. They also promote the complementary notion, that no-one outside the guild should or indeed could provide this service.

Local specialists and guilds have very different economic strategies. Local specialists like shamans and diviners are authoritative only in a particular place; the guild potentially covers any territory. Local specialists are supposed to be different by internal nature from other people; the guild describes its members as specially trained. A religious guild promises to deliver a stable, uniform kind of service that only it can provide, but also a service that any member of the guild will provide in the same way. Proper service depends not on the personal qualities of the specialists but on their being similar to any other member of the guild.

These differences also extend to the concepts each group puts forward. It is quite natural for a shaman to construe his locally recognized powers as a special connection to local supernatural agents. By contrast, specialists who endeavor to operate on a large market, naturally think of themselves as interacting with highly abstract, delocalized, cosmic gods. A local shaman tends to interact with social groups: a family, a lineage. His interventions are said to protect the bones of the lineage or restore a family's defiled honor. By contrast, guilds generally tend to garner help from central political power and consequently address not local groups but the individual. Hence their insistence on such notions as the individual soul, one's personal merit, one's salvation.

The kinds of religious concepts offered in the context of organized guilds are very different from those of local specialists, shamans and healers. Guilds tend to downplay intuition, divination, personal inspiration and orally transmitted lore because all these naturally fall outside the guild's control. True descriptions of supernatural agents are said to come in the form of a stable and general doctrine, rather than on-the-hoof, contextual solutions to specific problems. Regarding sacrifice for instance, a typical question in local religious activities is: "Will the ancestors be satisfied with this pig and help this child recover?" A typical one in a literate religion would be "What animals must be sacrificed for what types of illnesses?" and the answer to that is a general answer.

As a guild claims to offer similar services throughout a large polity, it cannot claim to have a particular connection to local supernatural agents, such as ancestors and local spirits. The agents that the institution claims to interact with must be such that any member of the guild, wherever they are, could be said to be in contact with them. This is one of the main reasons why such "small gods" and spirits are usually demoted in the doctrines of religious institutions and replaced with more general, cosmos-wide agents. Also, religious guilds tend to promote a very specific understanding of death and the destiny of various components of the person. What happens to the soul is presented as a consequence of general processes that apply to all humans. Religious guilds replace the intrinsically local notions of "establishing" the ancestors, turning them for instance into mountains or into the pillars of a house, with a general and abstract notion of salvation conditioned by moral behavior. Such a notion is found in most written religious doctrines, with important differences in how salvation is defined and what kind of morality is attached to such definitions. The Jewish and Christian versions imply proximity to God as well as a very vaguely defined (especially in the Jewish case) afterlife, while the Indian (Hindu or Buddhist) versions imply an exit from the cycle of reincarnations and the elimination of the soul as a self. These are among the variations on a theme found in many literate traditions. Death should not be construed only as a passage to the status of an ancestor but also as a radical leave-taking from society. This makes sense, as the doctrine is offered by specialists who have no particular service to offer in terms of local cults to local characters, or in any case nothing that could be seemingly better than the services of local shamans and other religious specialists.

Obviously, the special nature of the service they provide means that religious guilds cannot operate entirely in the same way as craftsmen's associations. There is of course no objective way to determine whether any religious provider is better than any other, whereas people can always observe that the trained and experienced cobbler makes better shoes than a novice. So, however strongly the guild may claim that its rites are the only way of obtaining particular results, people are fickle and may at any moment decide that some cheaper, home-made or shaman-offered recipe may be just as good. Because of that elusive quality of supernatural services, there is always harsh competition among suppliers. In most complex polities, an organized guild of religious practitioners is faced with a whole variety of informal providers, local shamans, wizards, healers, inspired idiots and ominous dreamers. In most cases, the guild uses whatever political or ideological clout it can garner to dissolve this competition, demote it, relegate it to unimportant or local rituals, hinder its operation or the transmission of its recipes. This can result in the elimination of the local specialists, or their confinement to a cultural underground, as in most places, or to a peaceful coexistence, as for instance in India and other places where one finds a combination of so-called "great" and "little" traditions. In general, the guilds' efforts to establish a monopoly are bound to fail in the long run, for the strength of informal practice is precisely that it is informal and can therefore be started anew at very low cost. As all religious specialists know, the war against what they tend to call superstition is never-ending.

As Hume noted, polytheistic heathens are far more tolerant than monotheistic priests.[4] People who follow particular ancestor cults or offer sacrifices to local spirits are generally indifferent to the religious behaviors or ideas of other communities. Even when they have the means to influence outsiders, they seem to lack the motivation to do so. Religious institutions, on the other hand, are invariably drawn to intolerance, to the refusal of other religious practices and to their extirpation though political influence. The main reason is a matter of marketing and of politics. Doctrines promoted by professional guilds and guilds depend on the stable and de-contextualized provision of similar services. Guilds are cartels. Groups of craftsmen the world over try to make prices and services uniform, and repress attempts to individualize services. In the same way, we know that members of religious guilds intuitively perceive that charismatic specialists dangerously threaten their group's overall grip on the market. The conflict is a political and economic one between individuals located in different niches of the religious market. This also explains why the opposition is always asymmetrical. The potential conflict between following the guild and following more local specialists is invariably highlighted by the guild's attempt to repress, suppress or downgrade the local specialists, not the other way around. In other words,

4 HUME, *Natural History of Religion* [1757], Section IX.

shamans are much more dangerous to priests than priests to shamans. The survival of a religious guild requires that some limits be set to what local specialists can provide.

It is quite natural for a local specialist to use flexible, highly variable ritual recipes, using his personal knowledge of situations and customers. A guild by contrast, trying to make most of its members interchangeable, is bound to insist on highly codified, inflexible ritual recipes. Because of all these requirements, members of religious guilds generally use literate codes and other texts to maintain uniform provision of religious services. Given that such guilds only appeared in complex polities and that these very often had some writing system, it is not surprising that the guilds also used writing. A great advantage of writing is that it facilitates the uniformity of service and practice that is the main selling point of such professional groups. So guilds that emphasize literate sources – written transmission and the kind of systematic argument made easier by writing – are more likely to subsist than groups that ignore the technology of writing. Conversely, given that uniformity and substitutability are important assets of the guild, any appeal to personal charismatic features or shamanistic revelation is actively discouraged. Incidentally, to say that guilds act against the competition, exert some coherent political influence, or maintain their predominance through the use of particular concepts does not mean that these social groups are agents. All it means is that most members of such groups tend to adopt a strategy of coalitional solidarity with the guild; social and political effects stem from these aggregated strategies.

Religions as brands

Given the elusive nature of the services they provide, literate groups of religious specialists always remain in a precarious position. The difficult training and special knowledge make sense and can subsist only if there is some guarantee that people will actually need the special services. One solution is to turn the guild's ministration into a *brand*, that is, a service that is (1) clearly distinct from what others could provide, (2) similar regardless of which member of the guild provides it, and (3) exclusively provided by one organization. A Catholic missionary offers rituals that are quite different from the ancestor-based rituals his African congregation were used to; but Catholic rituals are also quite stable from one priest to another; some observable features make it easy for most observers to distinguish between say a Catholic mass and what is offered by rival guilds. There is nothing intrinsically demeaning in saying that some services are offered in the form of a particular brand. This is likely to occur whenever an organized group of producers is in competition with both local, independent producers and rival organizations.

The creation of recognizable brands of religious services has important consequences for the kinds of concepts put forward by religious institutions.

Guilds offer an account of gods and spirits that is generally integrated (most elements hang together and cross-reference each other), apparently deductive (you can infer the guild's position on a whole variety of situations by considering the doctrine's general principles) and stable (you get the same message from all members of the guild). This last feature is particularly important for diffusion. Even complex concepts can gradually become more and more familiar to the illiterate masses through consistent sermons and recitations. How do the guilds manage to keep their message stable and uniform?

There is an extraordinarily high correlation between institutional religion and the presence of literacy. It would be difficult to find a literate polity without a doctrinal system or a doctrinal practice outside literate cultures. This may not be too surprising if we consider the general cognitive effects of literacy.[5]

These common social factors – the constitution of a cartel of religious specialists, its requirements in terms of uniformity and stability – explain the convergent features of many such religious groups: their insistence on cosmic questions rather than particular misfortune as the foundation of religious behavior, their notions of personal salvation as opposed to collective security, and more generally, the idea that religion requires a doctrine, that it is based on a doctrine, that its outward manifestations are consequences of the doctrine: all statements that make sense as the self-serving discourse of professionals, but should not bamboozle students of religion, whose job it is to explain religious thought and behavior as they actually occur, not as the guild wishes they did.

To sum up, then, it seems that "religion" – the assumption of a special domain of thought and behavior – was the invention of corporate groups, institutional guilds with property, recruitment services, the training of specialists and a large share in the provision of a whole range of services. The latter include rites of passage, ceremonies to promote fertility and eschew misfortune, discourse about superhuman agents, the enforcement of particular social norms and morality, sometimes the healing of sick people and often an explanation of and justification for existing political institutions. The domain comprised of all these services was called "religion" – it is therefore important to remember that there is little unity there, except that all these activities were now under the aegis of a single institution, the guild of religious officers.

---

5 See GOODY, *Literacy in Traditional Societies* [1968]; *The Domestification of the Savage Mind* [1977]; *The Logic of Writing and Organizing of Society* [1986].

Does the study of religion need "religion"?

If "religion" consists of diverse mental and social phenomena that actually belong to different domains of causation, it would seem to follow that the study of religious thought and behavior must consist in a catalog of different studies for different domains. If religious rituals belong to a study of ritualized behavior that has little to do with the study of supernatural imagination (as I will argue below); if such dissociations extend to other domains, then there is no promise and indeed no justification for an integrated "study of religion". However, this is not quite the standard position in the academic field of religious studies, despite vigorous debates about the usefulness of the category "religion". A classical assumption in the field is that there is something *sui generis* about religious phenomena. This position is best illustrated if we consider the terms used by such scholars such as Friedrich Schleiermacher or Rudolf Otto, as the former saw religious thought as a "sense and taste for the infinite" (Sinn und Geschmack fürs Unendliche) while the latter emphasized the *mysterium tremendum* and *mysterium fascinans* that supposedly accompanied religious thoughts.[6] To those scholars, religion was not just a special kind of thought, or of social phenomena, distinct from the rest – they also assumed that that the object of religion (gods, ancestors, spirits, etc.) was a separate level or domain of reality. This peculiar notion has not survived the development of the natural and social sciences. It is one thing to say that gods or ancestors, should they exist, would be made of different stuff than other objects in the world. It is quite another thing to assume that human thoughts about these objects should be of a different fabric than the rest of our mental life – or that religious social phenomena obey different laws from other aspects of society.

These simple observations led to the idea of a naturalistic study of religion – which is now the *de facto* world-view of most people who study religious thought and behavior as mental and social phenomena.[7] It is remarkable that this simple idea of a naturalistic study, which would strike most specialists of other social phenomena, like sports or politics or homicide or agriculture, as quite clearly self-evident, has been so contentious for such a long time in the study of religion.[8] A reason for this is the persistence of implicit apologetic agendas in the study of religion, an unsurprising phenomenon given the direct filiation between religious institutions and places of scholarship about religion. Donald Wiebe has analyzed and vigorously denounced the persistence of apologetic agendas in supposedly academic institutions, made all the more pernicious as it is *sub rosa*, as it were, and unconnected to overt religious

---

6 OTTO, *Das Heilige* [1920], 13, 43. SCHLEIERMACHER, *Über die Religion* [1799], 53.
7 See PREUS, *Explaining Religion* [1989].
8 See MCCUTCHEON, *Manufacturing Religion* [1997], vii-xii.

affiliation or commitment.[9] More surprising to the social scientist is the fact that some kind of general apologetic purpose, a defense of religiosity, as it were, rather than any specific religious doctrine, is still present in the study of religion. This was for instance, a crucial assumption in Eliade's work and that of his followers.[10]

Once dissipated the unnecessary ontology – religious thoughts and behaviors are not of a specific nature, different from all other thoughts and behaviors – we can focus on the more pressing question, how should one study religious thoughts and behavior? Does one require that "religion" and "religious" be part of our explanatory vocabulary? There are two ways of thinking about this. Some scholars, following Jonathan Z. Smith's recommendation, eschew any commitment to specific nature of religion, yet make use of the category "religion" as a mere description of a particular domain.[11] Others, like anthropologist Benson Saler, would use the term "religion" only in social contexts where there is such a category.[12] As I said above, the evidence would suggest that the study of religious phenomena does not need a notion of "religion" at all.

An uncertain and unnecessary concept

In the same way as there are such things as Madame Bovary's ennui and the unicorn's horn, there is such a thing as "religion" since enough people talk about it. But the question I raised here is, does that notion help us understand what goes on when people adhere to (or for that matter, discard belief in) supernatural beings? My answer is that the notion is extremely misleading. We understand better all these phenomena once we stop believing that they are *sui generis* and belong together.

Do trees exist? Or rather, does it make sense to think that there is something in common to all trees? This is not a metaphysical question that could be decided once and for all in the abstract, but a practical one that relates our concepts to what we want to understand about the world. For lumberjacks, landscape designers, geographers, architects, and indeed anyone who needs some shade (as well as for most non-human animals that climb trees, make nests or find shelter in fronds and foliage), it makes sense to think of trees as highly similar objects of the same kind, very different from grasses, bushes or brush. For evolutionary biologists and geneticists on the other hand, this makes no sense at all, because some trees are very close cousins of ferns, while

9 Wiebe, *The Politics of Religious Studies* [1998], 92–113.
10 See McMullin, *The encyclopedia of religion* [1989].
11 See Smith, *Imagining Religion* [1982].
12 See Saler, *Conceptualizing Religion* [1993].

others are much closer to other plants. With different explanatory goals, so changes the delineation of what things are really out there. Incidentally, this does not mean that "anything goes" and that what is or is not around us is up for us to decide. If you are a landscape architect or a hiker in search of shade, you simply have no choice but to consider trees as one kind of thing. If you are a biologist, you have no other option but to say that "tree" is a misleading category.

So whether there is such a thing as "religion" depends on what you want to do with all these behaviors and thoughts. For people who want other human beings to stay in contact with reality instead of living in metaphysical fantasy, it makes sense to think that there is such a thing as religion – and that there is too much of it around. For politicians who think policies should be grounded in rational argument, the notion makes sense.

But we are not engaged in these endeavors here. What we are trying to do is provide scientific explanations for the emergence and survival of the concepts and norms I summarized above. In this particular enterprise, it would be foolish to assume that there is such a thing as "religion", for the reasons I already outlined, and will specify in the following chapters. The notion assumes something that is precisely questionable, and in my view actually false, namely that there is something in common to religious thoughts and behaviors that would explain their emergence and survival. That particular assumption flies in the face of what we know about human psychology and the evolution of human cultures – but showing that obviously requires more argument and evidence.

The argument proposed here, which I think derives from the empirical evidence in a fairly straightforward manner, would suggest that all attempts at "explaining religion" are, to some extent, barking up the wrong tree, or fighting windmills – or in less metaphorical terms, simply misguided as there is nothing there to explain. Having a general explanation of "religion" is the same as having a general explanation for the evolution of trees – the scheme may be ingenious but it happens to "explain" something that is actually not the case. People have tried to explain religious beliefs in terms of infantile thought, as the flight of reason, as the need for explanations, the urge for reassurance, the necessity of social cohesion and the interests of patriarchy. All those things are real, but they are not the explanations, for the thing to be explained is largely an illusion fostered by religious guilds. Science can explain a lot about people's religious thoughts and behaviors, and should not concern itself with explaining what is non-existent.

2. What is natural in religions?

Philosophers and scholars of many different traditions have speculated on the existence of "natural religion", a set of religious thoughts and behaviors that we are likely to encounter in most human groups. I would argue that there is such a set, that some concepts and norms are represented by many people in most human groups because of the way human minds work. It does not mean that all these thoughts and behaviors are "natural" in the sense of being adaptive, as we will see presently. Nor does it imply, of course, that there is anything true or profound about these widespread notions. Error is just as "natural" as knowledge, indeed often more so. The fact that many minds converge toward a particular kind of notion only means that our minds are so organized, that they find it difficult to avoid it.

Natural religion as a theory

David Hume saw religious thoughts as natural consequences of human psychology. It followed that some religious notions, e. g. that of supernatural agency, would appear in normal human minds, as a result of their standard operation, with or without a specific revelation or tradition. This eminently sensible view was not well received at the time – but it marks the beginnings, at least in Europe, of a scientific project of explaining religion as the result of *natural* causes, social and psychological. Against Christian theologians who saw, e. g. ancient Jewish doctrine as far too sophisticated to be the invention of a few tribes, Hume had little difficulty showing that nothing in the religious repertoire of most societies is beyond naturalistic explanation.

The idea of a natural form of religious thought, a set of concepts or norms that will appear in any group because of the constitution of human minds and societies, is of course older than Hume, and important in many non-European traditions, too. In classical Islamic theology, eminent scholars disputed the status of religious beliefs, and particularly moral norms, in places and times that were either before or beyond Muhammad's revelation.[1] Would a man who lived either before Revelation or in lands beyond the umma, be committing a sin by drinking alcohol? That was debatable; but at the same time it seemed that the moral status of some actions, like lying to people or assaulting them, would have been clear even before revelation. In this way, some Muslim thinkers were implicitly considering that certain forms of

---

1 REINHART, *Before Revelation* [1995], 6 ff.

religion and morality may be natural to human beings, although the full development of these capacities would only be possible within the Islamic tradition.

For all these thinkers, and for the modern cognitive perspective on religion, "natural religion" obviously does not suggest a particular doctrine or tradition that would be the *fons et origo* of all other religions. For a long time, scholars in the history of religion considered shamanism to be the ancestor, *the* primitive religion in both senses: as the source of subsequent traditions and also as an unrefined or primal form of religiosity. Indeed, it seemed that some form of shamanism was found in most non-urban societies, with similar features – like the notions of spirits or souls, the idea that some privileged individuals have the capacity to visit the world of the spirits, the use of altered states of consciousness by many of these practitioners, and the assumption that many forms of illness and misfortune could be palliated by shamanistic intervention. These are indeed pretty common features around the world – indeed they are certainly present in modern, industrial societies in the form of mediums and healers. However, we should not be misled into thinking that there is such a thing as the shamanistic religion. In most places where shamanism exists, it is not institutionalized and has no specific doctrine; although people routinely use shamans to address some problems, somatic or otherwise, they are not especially committed to any specific notions of how these specialists operate.

What is the phenomenon?

What the term "religious" denotes is far from clear in contemporary anthropology and religious studies,[2] so it may be of help to start with a rough demarcation of the field of inquiry. I am here taking an evolutionary standpoint, and considering a large domain of behaviors that include the following:

(1) Mental representations of non-physical agents, including ghosts, ancestors, spirits, gods, ghouls, witches, etc., and beliefs about the existence and features of these agents.
(2) Artefacts associated with those mental representations, such as statues, amulets or other visual representations or symbols.
(3) Ritual practices associated with stipulated non-physical agents.
(4) Moral intuitions as well as explicit moral understandings that people in a particular group connect to non-physical agency.
(5) Specific forms of experience supposed to either bring about some proximity to non-physical agents or communicate with them.
(6) Ethnic affiliation and coalitional processes linked to non-physical agents.

Are there religious universals? Some of these features may well constitute

---

2 See SMITH, *Imagining Religion* [1982].

substantive cultural universals.[3] This however is not crucial to evolutionary models, whose aim is to explain the variance observed in terms of some common factors. This means that explanations should be sought for all cultural phenomena whose recurrence is not random.

In many domains, evolution resulted in dispositions that render humans sensitive to particular contextual input, but evolved human dispositions do not always result in uniform behaviors or cultural outputs.

Were such religious phenomena present in ancestral times? If they were influenced by natural selection, we should expect at least some of them to be both ancient and widespread. In the archaeological record, we find evidence for a variety of non-pragmatic behaviors, such as elaborate burial procedures, from the earliest stages of the Paleolithic age and perhaps also in Neanderthals. Most Paleolithic art was probably not about superhuman agents at all but concerned itself with more pressing issues such as sex and hunting.[4] But chimerical representations show that at least some supernatural concepts (see below for a precise definition) were present.[5] Did all this constitute some form of religious thought? The question only makes sense if we assume that "religion" stands for a natural kind, which is certainly not the case. More important, the archaeological evidence shows that many of the phenomena discussed here appear at the same point (about 50,000 years ago) along with other phenomena typical of modern humans, such as regional "cultural" differences, sophisticated tool-equipment, body ornamentation and make-up, and probably the first musical instruments. All evidence points to modern human minds and brains, quite similar to ours – which is why the evolutionary psychology of religious thought can make use of modern experimental studies of cognitive function.

The cognitive picture – supernatural concepts

A proper understanding of cultural phenomena should start with an understanding of the cognitive processes whereby cultural representations are acquired, stored, and transmitted. In the past fifteen years, various accounts of specific features of religion have converged to constitute what could be called a common or "standard" model of religious thought and behavior, based on the notion that religious concepts are a by-product of ordinary cognition.[6] This is the consequence of remarkable progress in

---

3 BROWN, *Human Universals* [1991], 130–141.
4 See GUTHRIE, *The Nature of Paleolithic Art* [2005].
5 See MITHEN, *The Prehistory of the Mind* [1996].
6 ATRAN, *In Gods we Trust* [2002], 12–13, 264–266; BARRETT, *Why Would Anyone Believe in God?* [2004]; BOYER, *The Naturalness of Religious Ideas* [1994]; LAWSON, E.T./MCCAULEY, *Rethinking Religion* [1990]; PYYSIÄINEN, *How Religion Works* [2001].

experimental psychology, developmental psychology, and cognitive neuro-science, which are converging towards a description of mental functioning as the operation of many different learning systems, each of which is geared to representing a particular domain of reality. As a result of these largely tacit learning principles, some types of representations and associations are intrinsically easier to acquire, remember, and communicate than others. This would suggest a fractionated model of religious cognition, in which different aspects of religious thought and behavior activate different mental capacities.[7] In this model, different kinds of religious thoughts "parasitize" cognitive structures that evolved for other, non-religious reasons.

This standard account starts from the notion of supernatural concepts. The world over, people's supernatural repertoire includes a variety of concepts of imagined artefacts, animals, persons, and plants: concepts of floating islands, of mountains that digest food or have blood circulation, of trees that listen, of animals that change species, or of people who can disappear at will. These are found in folktales, anecdotes, myths, dreams and religious ritual and correspond to a small "catalog" of templates for supernatural concepts. We also find that a particular subset of these concepts is associated with more serious commitment, strong emotions, important rituals, and/or moral understandings. An association between a supernatural concept and one or several of these social effects is our main intuitive criterion for what is "religious." In other words, religious cognitions are a subset of supernatural notions.

In the standard account, "supernatural" is defined in a precise way, which does not in any way assume that the people concerned entertain an elaborate notion of nature, such as for instance the Aristotelian Φυζις. Indeed, in most cultures in the world there is no explicit notion of the natural world and its limits. However, in most minds around the world, there are some precise implicit assumptions about natural processes, what we can call an intuitive ontology.[8] It is relative to those implicit understandings that some concepts can be called "supernatural", in particular relative to a set of ontological categories or "domain concepts" that we know are present in normal minds from an early stage of cognitive development.

There are, to simplify matters a great deal, two major levels of conceptual information in semantic memory. One is that of kind-concepts, notions like "table" and "tiger" and "tarmac" and "tree." The other consists of domain concepts, such as "intentional agent," "manmade object," "living thing." Most of the information associated with these broader concepts comes in the format, not of declared statements (e.g., "living things grow with age") but of intuitive expectations and inferences. Without being aware of it, one expects living things to grow, intentional agents to have goals, and their behavior to be

---

7 See BOYER, *The Naturalness of Religious Ideas* [1994].
8 See BOYER, *Natural epistemology* [2000].

caused by those goals, the structure of artefacts to be explained by a function, and the latter by a designer's intention. Objects in the environment are identified as belonging to kind categories ("telephone", "giraffe") but also to domain categories (PERSON, ARTEFACT, ANIMAL, etc.). We now have much better evidence concerning intuitive ontological categories and associated theories, coming from developmental psychology, from experimental studies with adults, from neuroscience and from the study of cognitive pathologies.

Concepts of imaginary objects and beings are intuitively associated with these ontological categories. The concept of spirit activates the category PERSON. If you pray to a particular statue of the Virgin, you are standing or kneeling in front of an ARTEFACT. If you think that some antelopes can disappear at will, you must activate your ANIMAL category to represent these special beings.

What is special about supernatural concepts is that they describe minimal *violations* of our intuitive expectations: a tree is said to listen to people's conversations, a statue is said to bleed on particular occasions, a person is described as being in several places at once, another one as going through walls, and so on. Note that such descriptions violate domain- and not kind-level expectations. A talking ebony tree goes against expectations not because ebony trees in particular are usually silent but because all plants are assumed to be non-intentional. Also, note that the violations are minimal, keeping in place all the (non-violated) default assumptions that usually accompany a given domain concept. A talking tree is still assumed to grow like all plants, ghosts that go though walls still perceive and represent their environment like other intentional agents. Indeed, these non-violated assumptions provide an indispensable grounding for people's inferences about supernatural entities and agents. This twofold condition: (1) include a violation of domain-level intuitions and (2) allow inferences from relevant non-violated assumptions, is sufficient to account for the recurrent features of supernatural concepts the world over. That is, the subject matter of fantastic imagination, dreams, folktales, and religion generally revolves around a small catalog of concepts built in that way.

The cognitive account stipulates that there is a limited *catalog of supernatural concepts* derived from ontological concepts such as person, living thing, man-made object. A spirit is a special kind of person, a magic wand a special kind of artefact, a talking tree a special kind of plant. Such notions are salient and inferentially productive because they combine (1) specific features that violate some default expectations for the domain with (2) expectations held by default as true of the entire domain. These combinations of explicit violation and tacit inferences are culturally widespread and may constitute a memory optimum.[9]

---

9 BARRETT/NYHOF, *Spreading non-natural concepts* [2001]; BOYER/RAMBLE, *Cognitive templates for religious concepts* [2001], 557–559.

The concepts may be very different from one place to another, but the templates are few, consisting of a combination of one particular domain-concept and one particular violation (e.g. "intentional agent" and "physical solidity" for the "ghost" concept). Also, experimental work in different cultures suggests that concepts built in this way are more likely to be recalled than either predictable conceptual associations, or oddities constructed by violating kind-level associations. A table made of sausages (violation of kind-level expectations) may be quite striking, but in the end is not quite as easily acquired and recalled as a table that understands conversations (violation of domain-level expectations). This effect seems to work in fairly similar ways in different cultural environments.

Why are supernatural concepts culturally stable?

What we generally call "religious" concepts, e.g. notions of gods, spirits, ancestors, are a subset of supernatural notions, with special additional features that we will describe presently. But it is worth insisting on the fact that they belong to this broader domain, as this explains their mode of acquisition. In supernatural concepts, most of the relevant information associated with a particular notion is given by domain-level intuitions. In other words, it is spontaneously assumed to be true in the absence of contrary information. This is why no one in the world needs to be told that ghosts see what happens when it happens, or that gods who want some result will try to do what it takes to achieve it: such inferences are given for free by our specialized mental systems (intuitive psychology in this case). In religion, as in other supernatural domains, the violations are made clear to people, but the rest is inferred. Concepts that are both salient (because of the violation) and very cheaply transmitted (because of spontaneous inferences) are optimal from the viewpoint of cultural transmission. Now some supernatural concepts matter much more than others. Whether Puss-in-boots did run faster than the wind or not is of no great moment, but whether the ancestors noticed that we offered them a sacrifice certainly is. The question is, why do some concepts of imagined entities and agents, rather than others matter to people? Because, I will argue, other specialized mental systems are involved in their representation. Religious concepts are associated with intuitions about agency, about social interaction, about moral understandings, and about dead bodies.

So let us look at the way supernatural concepts, including the "religious" ones, are transmitted. It is quite clear that religious concepts, just like fairy tales or urban myths, are good for cultural transmission, so to speak, since they seem to spread without the need for modern media, institutional support or individual effort. That is, acquiring the religious and supernatural notions of one's own cultural environment is an entirely effortless and generally successful acquisition process, which often results in the spread of roughly similar notions over vast regions and long periods. In the last twenty years, a number of psychologists have focused on the ways in which human memory may bias cultural evolution, making supernatural concepts particularly likely to survive multiple events of transmission.

We now have some experimental evidence that individual processes tend to favor supernatural concepts of the format described above. In a number of controlled studies, Justin Barrett and colleagues used artificial concepts that correspond to the templates described above, yet are not culturally familiar.[10] These studies measured recall for such concepts in the context of short narratives. Recall is particularly important because it is a necessary condition for cultural transmission. All else being equal, concepts that are recalled better than others have a higher potential for transmission. These studies showed that violations of intuitive expectations are recalled better than standard associations, that recall depends on ontological violations, not just on oddity, and that it requires background default expectations. Intuitive expectations that are not violated are the main source of inferences about supernatural situations.

This was demonstrated for instance by Barrett and Keil's ingenious experiments on God concepts.[11] They elicited from the participants features that, in their view, made God special. Subjects generally mentioned violations of theory-of-mind expectations, for example that God attends to everything at once. They then tested recall for stories that used these violations. They found that in the subjects' recall such features were generally replaced with more intuitive descriptions of cognitive functioning, taken from our spontaneous "theory of mind". Such sensitivity to violations is cross-culturally stable. Barrett replicated for instance his God concept studies in India with similar results, and Boyer and Ramble did it in two contrasted settings in Gabon and in Nepal.[12] Supernatural notions are, more than other concepts, "fit" for recall and transmission from individual to individual because they are attention-grabbing and allow further thoughts.

---

10 See BARRETT, *Anthropomorphism, Intentional Agents, and Conceptualizing God* [1996], *Cognitive constraints on Hindu concepts of the divine* [1998]; BARRETT/NYHOF, *Spreading non-natural concepts* [2001]; BOYER/BEDOIN/HONORE, *Relative contributions from kind- and domain concepts* [2001]; BOYER/ RAMBLE, *Cognitive templates for religious concepts* [2001].

11 See BARRETT/KEIL, *Conceptualizing a nonnatural entity* [1996].

12 See BOYER/RAMBLE, *Cognitive templates for religious concepts* [2001].

The cognitive picture – non-physical agency

The supernatural catalog includes all sorts of notions: artefacts with biological properties (e. g. statues that bleed), animals with a non-standard biology (e. g. chimeras and monsters), natural objects with odd physics (like the Flying Dutchman's vessel) and so on. But the important concepts, the ones that become the object of intense interest, the ones we think of as "religious", are invariably about non-physical agents. One possible explanation is that human minds are generally prone to anthropomorphic projections.[13] That is certainly a powerful tendency in human imagination – but in this case one must note that the projection of human features is selective. Only the *mental* properties of human beings are projected as the foundation of god- and spirit-concepts. Other properties of humans are less relevant, it would seem. So what is so compelling in the notions of agents with standard, human-like minds and non-physical existence?

It is certainly relevant that a good deal of human existence consists in interaction with agents that are not physically present – and that this is one of the major cognitive capacities that made humans a very special kind of primates. Many, perhaps most, of our thoughts about other people occur when they are not around. Memories of what people did or said, as well as expectations, fears and hopes of what they may do, are a constant theme of trains of thought and ruminations, and also the quintessential subject matter of gossip. In all human groups, people also fantasize about individuals they have not encountered yet (e. g. Mr. Right). They also entertain thoughts and emotions about deceased individuals, and about persons they will never encounter, like fictional characters. It may be a special feature of the human mind that we can create such representations and more importantly run rational inferences about them. It is certainly a central capacity of human thinking, appears early, is universal and distinctive of normal human minds. Perhaps this feature of spontaneous man imagination is less surprising given human capacities for "mind-reading" or "theory of mind", geared to interpreting other agents' (or one's own) behavior in terms of goals, beliefs, memories and inferences.[14]

But why should we have this capacity? From an evolutionary standpoint, there are two reasons not to develop a capacity to think about absent agents. First, such thoughts take time and energy away from consideration of present people. Second, they often result in fantasy-reality confusions, as we know from the experimental literature. A solution may be that thoughts about absent agents are necessary and useful given the computational constraints of social interaction. The capacity is of great evolutionary advantage, given the human

---

13 See GUTHRIE, *Faces in the Clouds* [1993].
14 ZUNSHINE, *Why We Read Fiction* [2006], 6–16.

dependence on social interaction. Humans live in a "cognitive niche", in that they more than any other species depend on information, especially on information provided by other human beings, and on information about other human beings.[15] This dependence means that mental dispositions that help maintain rich and flexible representations of others, of their goals and their mental states are crucial. Social interaction presents us with a whole gamut of possible actions from our partners as well as possible reactions to our own behavior. Reactions on our part should be fast but also appropriate. The potential cost of mismanagement of social relations is huge for humans, given their dependence on cooperation for survival. Now there is a trade-off between speed and appropriateness, given the complexity of inferences required for even the simplest social interaction. What each actor did or said may convey several intentions, to which there may be several possible responses, and so on. One way to bypass this computational hurdle may be to have a prepared catalog of possible interaction scenarios. These would be constructed when the other agent is not around, which would allow sluggish explicit inferences and the slow comparison of different scenarios in terms of plausibility. These scenarios would include appropriate responses. They could be tagged in memory in such a way that they can be quickly activated in actual interaction and provide an intuitive guide to apposite behavior. There is some preliminary evidence for the preparation and use of such scenarios in actual social behavior.[16]

Another salient case of a common domain of productive imagination is the frequent creation of imaginary friends by young children. From an early age (between three and ten) many children (perhaps more than half of them) engage in durable and complex relationships with such agents. These imagined persons or personified animals, sometimes but not always derived from stories or cartoons or other cultural folklore, follow the child around, play with her, converse with her, etc. Young children know perfectly well that their invisible companions are not "there" in the same sense as real friends and other people.[17] Now Marjorie Taylor has shown that the relationship with an imagined companion is a stable one, so the child must compute the companion's reactions, taking into account not just the imagined friend's personality but also past events in their relationship. What the companion does or says is constrained by their personality and must remain consistent and plausible even in this fantastic domain. Also, companions are often used to provide an alternative viewpoint on a situation. They may find odd information unsurprising or frightening situations manageable. So imaginary

15 Tooby/DeVore, *The reconstruction of hominid behavioral evolution through strategic modelling* [1987], 209 ff.
16 Malle/Moses/Baldwin, *Intentions and Intentionally* [2001]; Saarni, *Cognition, context, and goals* [2001].
17 See Taylor, *Imaginary Companions and the Children Who Create Them* [1999].

companions may constitute a form of training for the social mind, helping build the social capacities required to maintain coherent social interaction.[18]

In many human groups supernatural agency is associated with moral understandings. This may take the form of explicit moral codes supposedly laid down by gods or ancestors, or stories of exemplary semi-mythical ethical paragons. More generally, people assume that supernatural agents keep a watch on them and are concerned about moral behavior. A cognitive-evolutionary account may explain why this latter assumption is "natural" enough to be found in non-literate groups but also in the spontaneous religious thinking of most religious believers.[19]

Also central to our intuitive definition of things religious is the perform-ance of rituals, more or less directly connected to beliefs about non-physical agents. Ritualized behaviors are intuitively recognizable by their stereotypy, rigidity, repetition, and apparent lack of rational motivation. They range from private ceremonies with few participants, or indeed just one person, to large gatherings, and from single acts to long sequences spread over months or years. The general themes range from worship to protection to aggression. The occasions for ritualized behaviors also vary, either contingencies such as illness or misfortune, life-stages like birth, initiation, and death, or recurrent occasions such as seasonal changes.

Finally, many forms of religious activity constitute precautionary behaviors against real but unobservable dangers, yet a recurrent finding is that the actions prescribed seem to have little direct causal connection to the result desired; no intermediate mechanism is represented.[20] This may not be so surprising, given that magical prescriptions typically effect changes on invisible objects, such as sources of contamination or other people's mental states. Indeed, this may be a general feature of precautionary thinking. In the domains of contagion, predation, or social relations, people are prepared to accept as plausibly efficacious recipes whose causal mechanisms are opaque.[21] Magical associations also frequently activate social cognitive capacities, particularly in the representation of misfortune. People assume that ancestors or gods are involved in various occurrences (bad crops, illness, death, etc.).

18 See TAYLOR/CARLSON, *The relation between individual differences in fantasy and theory of mind* [1997].
19 See BOYER, *Functional origins* [2000].
20 See SØRENSEN, "The morphology and function of magic" *revisited* [2002].
21 FIDDICK, *Domains of deontic reasoning* [2004], 568–472.

Natural religion is not (just) for the primitive Other

We commonly call "religions" two rather disparate sets of objects. There is a set of so-called "world religions" or doctrines of great diffusion, such as Judaism, Buddhism or Islam. There is also what anthropologists, when they are in the mood for categorization, call "traditional" religions: beliefs and practices that are firmly rooted in some local social relations, with little explicit theology and no corporation or guild of religious officers. For many understandable reasons, scholars of religion have generally established their base-camp in a thorough knowledge of "world religions". From this starting point they then tried to climb all the way up to a general understanding of religion in human kind. This however was not always very successful, despite the many new and fascinating vistas opened to scholarly exploration.

This was probably unavoidable. Studying doctrinal religions is all too likely to lead one onto a false trail, as far as religious thought and behavior are concerned. This is because doctrinal, so-called "world" religions are a secondary, derivative development of a much more general and deeply human tendency to imagine important supernatural agents, to entertain precise descriptions of their powers, and to establish social relations with these imagined agents. Without an understanding of this general mental disposition one does not understand much to the special case of "religions" armed with official personnel, some theologians, an important economic role and an affinity for political power.

Another, more damaging error is just as common and even more damaging. It consists in thinking that some societies or groups happen to have "world" or "organized religion" and others have what would be generally called "traditional religion", in the same way as some people are nomadic and others sedentary. The contrast is misguided because so-called "organized" religion, with explicit doctrine and specialized personnel, never *displaces* the other kind; it only *supplements* it. It is an add-on, an extra layer, an additional growth. What anthropologists usually describe as "traditional" religion is based on ways of thinking – about supernatural agents, about their interest in moral action, about their responsibility in human misfortune, etc. – that we find in all human groups. True, in some societies (including the ones most readers of this book belong to) there is also a totally different, integrated, explicitly argued notion, produced and fostered by specialists gathered in corporate associations. But this, the evidence suggests, does not really change much to most people's intuitive adherence to the more common ways of thinking. Many Christians probably think that, as far as religion is concerned, their minds are filled with Christian doctrine, or at least with notions and norms derived from Christian teachings. Most religious professional, as it were, priests, ministers, and theologians maintain a similar belief. Many students of religion also believe this. But nothing could be further from the truth. Doctrinal religion is a veneer that certainly covers, often conceals non-doctrinal concepts but which would not hold without the underlying material. Indeed, people's adherence to the doctrine actually requires intuitive, generally unconscious ways of thinking that stray far from the doctrine and in some cases contradict it.

This, incidentally, was anticipated by David Hume, writing about the flux and reflux of religious notions, between monotheism and polytheism. Hume was not talking about large religious institutions that adhere to either of these forms of religious ontology, but about the flux of such ideas in people's minds. In Hume's scenario, interaction with imagined agents requires that people give them "exaggerated praise and compliments". There seem to be two main reasons for that. First, even in highly polytheistic environments, people often tend to focus most of their religious attention on a few particular spirits or gods or even one of them, a kind of privileged religious partner, in the same way as people in early market societies tend to prefer trading with one privileged partner rather than explore an entire market.[22] Second, there is a tendency, and indeed there is an emotional incentive, to exaggerate the power of superhuman agents, as they represent an insurance against misfortune and an explanation for it, too. These two processes, if we follow Hume, would lead people towards quasi-monotheistic ideologies. However, equally strong cognitive constraints should push people away from monotheism towards what Hume called "idolatry". In particular, people need manageable super-human personnel – that is, gods and spirits that are not too distant. The institutions that foster notions of transcendent gods are therefore creating a niche for the cults of saints, ghosts, ancestors and other intermediaries. This process of flux and reflux is all too familiar to many religious officers, who lament the ever-present tendency of all congregations to move away from orthodoxy towards peripheral cults. No-one knows this better than pastors, rabbis or *ulema* trying to defend conceptually pure versions of their religious metaphysics against the tide of popular distortions.

Probabilistic, experience-distant model

All the propositions of the cognitive model are general, probabilistic and experience-distant. They are "general" in the sense that they could apply to any cultural milieu. Indeed, most explanatory accounts of religious concepts in cognitive terms make very little mention of the particular norms or practices that make one religious community different from the others. The way super-human agency is derived from ordinary assumptions about agency, for instance, is a cognitive process that may be found in Italian Catholics as

22 See POSNER, *A Theory of Primitive Society* [2001].

well as Korean shamans. Cognitive accounts are also "probabilistic". The fact that a given religious concept is easily acquired and recalled, salient and inferentially rich, all these features explain why, all else being equal, the likelihood increases that such a concept will be imagined and, once imagined, successfully transmitted in a particular cultural milieu. Finally, cognitive accounts are "experience-distant" – using a common anthropological term for explanatory accounts whose terms do not easily map onto people's own experiences. We describe religious concepts (gods, spirits, etc.) as only partly accessible to conscious inspection. The processes that make them salient or memorable, and lead the mind to particular expectations, are also outside awareness. Some social scientists may consider that we should also strive to make the model more historically specific. What this would mean, in practice, is this: We would take some predictions of the general cognitive models, and see to what extent the presence of particular cultural or historical factors changes likelihoods, makes certain outcomes more probable than others. For instance, we could contrast two behaviors that make super-natural agency more palpable, through a medium's trance or through an initiation rite. We could then specify political conditions under which each of these is more likely, and measure the success of such predictions against observed religious institutions. More generally, what we would do is gradually add factors to the general likelihood function of religious concepts and norms, and measure to what extent each addition reduces the overall behavioral variance to explain. This too is a sound strategy in all empirical sciences, particularly in their more applied domains. In the case of religion, this enterprise is all the more necessary as there is a clear social value in understanding, not just why there is religion in the first place, but also why it often takes forms that make social interaction difficult, dangerous or impossible. One could not be content with theories of religion that explain the attraction of super-human agency, but have nothing to say about why people spend time and effort in rituals, why many people in the world are so concerned about other people's beliefs, and why some are prepared to oppress or massacre others on apparently religious grounds.

What makes religious notions culturally viable

A central assumption in our cognitive account is that culturally widespread notions and norms are the result of a constant process of modification and transmission. This selectionist model implies that cultural distribution is simply the aggregate of many individual processes of acquisition and storage of information. Cultural information, however "traditional", is not and has never been stable. It is subject to incessant addition, deletion and distortion that occur in individual minds. Those particular sets of representations that we find recurrent between different people, between generations and across different groups are simply those which better than others resist change and distortion through innumerable processes of acquisition, storage, inference and communication. This may be because they constitute local "attractors", that is, optimal activation of particular mental resources.

It is very likely that by the time modern humans came out of Africa, they had the kind of supernatural imagination that founds religious concepts. It is quite certain that this imagination was active by the time of the "cultural explosion", the sudden emergence of cultural artefacts that show both great innovations and the beginnings of cultural style. It is also clear that dead bodies were the object of much special preparation by that time, being left adorned, accompanied with various artefacts or laid down to rest in special positions. We do not know whether those people also associated dead bodies with concepts of supernatural agents. To sum up, the kind of concepts and practices that we find the world over seems to appear right at the same time as all the mental capacities that are typical of the modern human mind.

Should we consider the "natural" part of religious thought described here as a biological adaptation? We will discuss in chapter 3 the view that religious morality may be seen as an evolutionary innovation. For the time being, focusing on concepts, it would seem that another explanation is possible that makes religious thought the fairly predictable by-product of mental capacities that would have appeared anyway. As I said above, most features of superhuman concepts seem to be fairly simple "tweakings" of ordinary conceptual and inferential capacities that we find in all human minds. For instance, the capacity to represent non-actual states of affairs and to draw consequences for such representations grounds people's perception of their past as well as their deliberation about future action. Developing such a capacity is a major evolutionary event; as a minor consequence, it also allowed one to imagine supernatural agents. In a similar way, the extraordinary complexity of human "theory of mind" (one's intuitive explanation of others and own behavior in terms of intentions and beliefs) was a major development that resulted in uniquely complex social interaction; it also allowed people to entertain complex thoughts about interaction with imagined agents. Modern humans also have an instinctive fear of invisible contaminants (like the pathogens of rotting bodies, blood, feces, etc.) and an intuitive notion of invisible contagion; such a cognitive adaptation is of great value. It also allows, as a by-product, the development of notions of invisible power ("the sacred", "taboo", "pollution", etc.) that we find in religious imagination, as we will describe in chapter 4.

Obviously, the fact that people entertain religious thoughts at all can have important consequences which we sometimes mistake for the explanation of religion. Once people find their imagined agents plausible, they can use them at times to allay anxiety like more pliable versions of real agents; once the versions of imagined agents differ from one culture to another, they can be used as convenient ethnic markers; once rituals are organized, a willingness to undergo gruesome ordeals can work a signal of commitment to the group. However, people did not create religion to allay their fears, first because it does not and second because people cannot create just any convenient fantasy and find it plausible. People did not create religion to foster good morality and group solidarity, because such a strategy would be vulnerable to defectors and quickly unravel.

We are left with a conclusion that many evolutionary biologists would find unsurprising – and most students of religion unpalatable: that religion is like dancing, music, ethnocentrism or body-ornaments: something that most humans are very good at learning and almost incapable of resisting, may sometimes have important consequences, yet has no other explanation than the quirks of the way evolution made our brains. What may make all this unpleasant or unacceptable to some people is the belief that important phenomena should have important causes, or at least their own, special causes. But cognitive models suggest that religious cognition is not really special and requires no special mental process, no exceptional evolutionary event.

3. Do religions make people better?

A familiar account and defense of institutionalized religions is that their function, or at any rate their consequence, is to create moral norms. C.S. Lewis for instance made morality an important step in what he thought of as a series of apologetic arguments. In his *Mere Christianity*, a carefully laid-out series of rational inferences happened to converge, by some happy coincidence, with the teachings of Protestant Christianity that were familiar in his cultural environment.[1] Unbeknownst to Lewis, that peculiar line of reasoning had been lampooned more than a century before, in Mr. Thwackum's famous statement in *Tom Jones*:

When I mention Religion, I mean the Christian Religion; and not only the Christian Religion, but the Protestant Religion; and not only the Protestant Religion, but the Church of England.[2]

Lewis's moral argument was that utilitarian considerations could of course tell us what is advantageous or disadvantageous for us, but not transform that into a notion of right or wrong. For that step, some metaphysical notion (indeed the one he happened to believe in) was required. The two parts of that argument are familiar from earlier philosophy – that intuitions of right and wrong are not derived from mere statements of positive or negative consequences is at least as old as Plato, and that morals may be the only reasonable justification of metaphysics, however unreasonable its claims, is of course Kant's conclusion. Obviously, both Plato and Kant were rather more sophisticated in their view of the matter, and both suggested that morality may well be connected to metaphysical claims, but certainly does not derive from them. That religious beliefs leads to virtue, and unbelief to depravity, is indeed a *locus communis* in religious apology. As Bentley put it most eloquently:

And if Atheism should be supposed to become universal in this nation [...] farewell all ties of friendship and principles of honor; all love for our country and loyalty to our prince; nay, farewell all government and society itself, all professions and arts, and conveniences of life, all that is laudable or valuable in the world.[3]

Bentley probably stated this so forcefully, indeed with such stridency, that he could perceive the inherent weakness of the claim. After all, voyagers had for a long time trailed the seven seas, and brought back many detailed accounts of

---

1 LEWIS, *Mere Christianity* [1997].
2 FIELDING, *The History of Tom Jones* [1749], 133.
3 BENTLEY, *The Folly of Atheism* [1692], 34.

exotic folks' customs. The overall picture of distant cultures that had gradually accumulated all the way from Herodotus and Ibn Batuta to the great voyages of the Renaissance, despite the travelers' predilection for the exotic, suggested that moral prescriptions were greatly similar in most places – Christian or not, indeed "religious" or not. Indeed, the very emphasis on odd or bizarre customs only reinforced the point. As Jean-Jacques Rousseau pointed out, even the apparent cases of straightforward moral violations did not override the general impression:

Should some peculiar and uncertain habits, grounded in local reasons unknown to us, ruin the inductive conclusion from the consensus of all people – who agree on nothing else but this particular point? O Montaigne, since you pride yourself on your candor and love of truth, be sincere and true, if a philosopher can, and tell me in what country on earth it is a crime to keep one's word, to be compassionate, benevolent, generous; where the virtuous man is despised and the scoundrel revered?[4]

That similarity, for Rousseau and many other European thinkers, was suggestive of some universal moral disposition, with many variations in the scope and expression of the capacity. This, indeed, was the view confirmed by most anthropological studies in the centuries that followed. Although there were plenty of immoral people, and certainly shocking differences in what counted as acceptable behavior, the fundamental moral intuitions seemed so similar that they were almost transparent.

The connection between morality and established institutional religion was dealt another serious blow, as far as European thinkers were concerned, by their discovery of Chinese culture – a brilliant civilization, technically and politically more advanced than the European nations – where morality was not based on religious thought, where indeed "religion" in the European sense was largely absent. The entire Chinese social order seemed to be founded on classical notions of morality without intervention of superhuman agency or supernatural imagination. Ever since the famous controversies about the role of the Jesuits in China, would-be proselytizers who discovered a rather more powerful conceptual system than the one they wished to impose on their hosts, the Chinese case undermined a standard assumption of European religious guilds, that their ministration was the only possible guarantee of public and private morality.

Having thus discarded an implausible account of morality, early Enlightenment thinkers now had to address the much more fundamental and difficult question, where does morality come from? It could not stem from fear or

---

4 ROUSSEAU: "Quelques usages incertains et bizarres fondés sur des causes locales qui nous sont inconnues, détruiront-ils l'induction générale tirée du concours de tous les peuples, opposés en tout le reste, et d'accord sur ce seul point? O Montaigne! toi qui te piques de franchise et de vérité, sois sincère et vrai si un philosophe peut l'être, et dis-moi s'il est quelque pays sur la terre où ce soit un crime de garder sa foi, d'être clément, bienfaisant, généreux ; où l'homme de bien soit méprisable, et le perfide honoré." Èmile [1762], 588–589.

coercion, therefore had to be among those mental dispositions that normally develop in human minds. Both Adam Smith and David Hume saw the origin of moral behavior in moral feelings, and the origin of those in the human capacity for empathy, for vicarious experience of some other person's feelings or pain.[5] As I will show presently, these two points are, more or less in the same form, the main conclusions of the scientific study of moral cognition – and they show how the classical apologetic had it diametrically wrong. Religions do not create moral understandings – the latter develop very well without religious thought.

Humans are "prosocial"

Humans are special in many ways, among which the extraordinary range and importance of cooperation in their interaction. Cooperation between non-genetically related individuals is rare in nature, and coordinated action involving more than two parties is also exceptional. But these and other forms of cooperation come natural to human beings. A whole literature, combining genetics, game-theory, paleontology and comparative psychology is dedicated to explaining this in terms of natural selection. I will not review this vast domain here but only highlight aspects of cooperation relevant to the issue at hand.[6]

More than any other species, humans depend on information from others and cooperation with others. Social interaction consists in an endless series of behaviors that do not seem "opportunistic", that is, geared to maximizing our immediate advantage. Because this is the natural milieu in which we live, social cooperation is "transparent" to us – only occasional departures from it make us realize that it is actually so widespread. In modern conditions, we routinely give tips in restaurants that we will not visit again, or help perfect strangers find their way. As important as what happens is what does not. We do not usually try to steal from others or cheat on them, we do not spend our time trying to shirk from work or exploit others – again, it is the exceptions we notice, and precisely because they diverge from the normal expectation.

Prosocial behaviors also manifest themselves in the human propensity to form social groups and coalitions with what anthropologists call "strong reciprocity", typically within small ethno-linguistic groups, or within modern nations that mimic the language of tribal affiliation (common ancestry territory, mores, etc.).[7] The specific norms of the community become the

5 See HUME, *A Treatise of Human Nature* [1739]; SMITH, *The Theory of Moral Sentiments* [1767].
6 See BOYD/RICHERSON, *Solving the puzzle of human cooperation* [2006]; GINTIS, *Strong reciprocity and human sociality* [2000], for surveys.
7 See BOYD/RICHERSON, *Solving the puzzle of human cooperation* [2006]; GINTIS, *Strong reciprocity and human sociality* [2000], for surveys.

object of great emotional commitment, and norm violations trigger punitive attitudes.[8] This disposition is also manifest in the innumerable coalitions that people constitute, from office cliques to political parties, from school coteries to vast social movements. We generally tend to see the negative sides of this, the feuds and vendettas and apparently irrational ethnic strife, but these are only the flip side of the cooperative coin, of human "groupishness", the disposition to commitment to and solidarity with the group, often at great risk.[9]

Finally, as Rousseau pointed out in the above quotation, we cannot find a human group where people do not routinely evaluate the moral aspects of behavior, however diverse their specific moral prescriptions. In all human groups, moral judgments are generally accompanied by moral feelings, by specific emotions like outrage, disgust, pride and admiration, that focus on the moral qualities of other people's and one's own behaviors.

That humans are so cooperative, especially in situations where no benefit could possibly be gained from that attitude, has long been a mystery to economists, as such behaviors seem to deviate from the maximization of utility. For a long time, the standard reaction was to dismiss them as irrational and in any case economically marginal. However, a wealth of data from experimental economics have shown that other-regarding tendencies are general and stable, while economists have observed that these tendencies operate even in supposedly rational markets. Economic theory now includes various types of models for the stability of cooperation norms. These can be combined with evolutionary models to account for the appearance of cooperation norms, but also of moral feelings.

Apparently, morality could not possibly evolve

The human tendency to engage in peaceful, non-competitive social cooperation is certainly advantageous – but how could it occur? Our spontaneous answer would be a functionalist one – it occurs because that is what makes social interaction possible, and we depend on social interaction for our survival – accompanied by a developmental scenario – human beings are not born cooperators, they become so because of cultural pressure. In more specific terms, cultural elders like parents but also members of the larger community ensure that developing children acquire the proper cooperative attitudes. Disapproval and punishments well as positive sanctions ensure the

---

8 See Price/Cosmides/Tooby, *Punitive sentiment as an anti-free rider psychological device* [2002].
9 Ridley, *The Origins of Virtue* [1996], 39 f.

gradual acquisition, or "internalization" of social norms, including moral ones, until they become for us a value in themselves.

There is an element of truth in the scenario. Cooperation is a good thing, indeed an indispensable condition, for the survival of groups and individuals. Members of social groups do ensure that norms are enforced and violators sanctioned. Children do have different moral intuitions from adults. However, as an explanation for the appearance of all these behaviors in human beings, this functionalist and developmental scenario is hopelessly inadequate. This is because of the way dispositions and behaviors appear in the context of natural selection.

In biological evolution, features evolve if they provide some fitness advantage in the context of a particular environment of evolution. The raw material of evolutionary processes is variation. No variation, no natural selection. There must be some variety among a species, for selective pressures to affect some organisms more than others, and therefore make some variants more frequent than others in a population. The giant anteaters' ancestors can only develop their efficient long snout because, at each point in their history, there was enough variation in nose lengths to create inequality in fitness, to the advantage of longer-snouted individuals.[10] This is true for complex behaviors too. The ingenious ways in which many birds avoid, mislead or harass predators could only evolve because different individuals performed them in ever so slightly different ways, making some individuals more successful than others.[11] Another property of evolution is that it is blind to future developments, as these examples also illustrate. Anteaters did not develop longer snouts because at some future point it would be highly beneficial to have them. The snouts were selected because at each point the longer version was more advantageous than the shorter one.

The cognitive capacities and motivations involved in cooperation are highly specific. Motives for social cooperation are different from those engaged in e.g. foraging, predator-prey relations or reproduction. For these reasons, cooperation (where it exists) is supported by specific capacities and motivations. In other words, the gradual fine-tuning of cooperation over many generations requires genetic selection of alleles such that normal brains developing in normal environments will comprise the capacities and motivations described above. Neuro-scientific and evolutionary evidence converge to suggest that one of the many specificities of a human brain lies in neuro-circuitry supporting exchange.[12]

In this as in other domains, evolution creates motivational proxies for adaptive fitness. People do not for instance engage in sex because that is the most direct way to spread their genes, but because of the anticipation of

10 See Delsuc et al., *The evolution of armadillos, anteaters sloths* [2001].
11 See Wheatcroft/Price, *Reciprocal cooperation in avian mobbing* [2008].
12 See Cosmides/Tooby, *Neurocognitive Adaptions Designed for Social Exchange* [2005].

pleasure. In the same way, they do not engage in prosocial behaviors because these are ultimately adaptive or even because they are in some sense beneficial. Indeed, the benefits of cooperation often take a long time to become apparent. So people cooperate rather than defect because of strong emotion-based preferences. They do not calculate that it would be a bad idea to mug the little old lady, take all her money and run. They feel that that is a repulsive proposition, a point I will emphasize presently.

In this perspective, the evolution of prosociality appears improbable and indeed mysterious. As we said, exchange and cooperation are highly beneficial. But that is not sufficient to create the selective pressure for their emergence, and makes their persistence problematic. Consider the latter problem. We have a species where individuals are generally disposed to cooperate with each other, therefore reaping all the individual benefits of cooperation. Now, since most dispositions come with some variations, some individuals may be less inclined to cooperate than others. Game-theoretic models, and also commonsense, predict that such reluctant cooperators will proliferate in the population, since they reap the benefits of overall high levels of sociality, yet do not contribute to the group as much as others. This would make the population in general slightly less disposed to cooperation after a few generations. But then, the process will iterate itself again, favoring an even lower degree of cooperation. Barring other selective pressures, the population should rapidly reach the equilibrium of no cooperation at all. This also explains why we should not expect "cooperative genes" (or rather gene-complexes) to appear and get selected to start with.

Incidentally, that is also why we should not trust our common intuition, that prosocial behavior can be gradually instilled in reluctant children by a combination of coaxing and coercion. That is rather unlikely for many reasons that we will explore presently, but the main one is that this scenario assumes that we have a disposition to be convinced or swayed by that coaxing and coercion. But that disposition will probably occur in varying degrees in different individuals providing a convenient niche for those who are less disposed to be taught.

All this explains why the first evolutionary accounts of evolved cooperation focused on highly specific circumstances, in which the individual adaptive advantage is straightforward. First, *kin-selection* favors the evolution of behaviors that benefit related organisms (e. g. bees working for their queen) inasmuch as they increase the organism's inclusive fitness.[13] Second, some animals can engage in *reciprocal altruism* (also known as "you scratch my back, I'll scratch yours"), whereby they can exchange favors with non-relatives, under strict conditions of reciprocation.[14] Even this minimal form of cooperation, however, is rare in nature as it requires complex cognitive

---

13 See HAMILTON, *The general evolution of social behaviour* [1964].
14 TRIVERS, *The evolution of reciprocal altruism* [1971].

systems. To avoid exploitation, animals that engage in such reciprocal exchange must maintain a store of memories for sharing situations, as well as distinct memories for different conspecifics and some appreciation of each other's capacity and willingness to reciprocate. The cost of developing such dedicated neural machinery must remain below potential benefits from reciprocity. But the cost-benefit calculation, in some circumstances, favors the selection of such dispositions.

However, cooperation in human beings does not reduce to either nepotism or reciprocal altruism. Reciprocal altruism, for instance, simply requires one to recall which individuals cooperated and which defected, together with a disposition to return the favor. However, human cooperation is more altruistic than expected utility would predict. This disposition to cooperate is manifest in economic games and everyday behaviors.[15] Such behaviors are bound to remain mysterious until we find out how they can contribute to individual fitness, despite the obvious opportunities they offer to cheats and free-riders.

Models of commitment

Most cooperation is difficult because it requires that one abandon some advantage. To compound the difficulty, any possible advantage of cooperation lies in the future, while the sacrifices it entails are (in general) to be made right away. Conversely, failing to cooperate may bring about negative outcomes, but that too generally happens in the future. We know that "what goes around comes around", but precisely, it comes after it went. For instance, helping one's colleagues may well make them more pleasant in the future, but the loss of one's time is immediate. Conversely, stealing the little old lady's purse brings a positive reward now and a negative one later in the form of a possible prison sentence. But that is *later*.

Now one of the most general psychological principles is that later counts for less than now, in other words that people like all other animals engage in temporal discounting. The value of future rewards is always discounted by a specific factor, the discount rate, and the slope of the discount curve tells us to what extent the expectation of time-delayed rewards can drive behavior.[16] Discount rates can be studied experimentally by presenting subjects with choices between rewards of various values to be expected at various times. These studies show how the discount curves are affected by such factors as age

15 See FRANK, *Cooperation through emotional commitment* [2001]; SMITH, *Constructivist and ecological rationality in economics* [2003].

16 See AINSLIE, *Précis of breakdown of will* [2005]; LOEWENSTEIN/READ, *Time and Decision* [2003], 635–650.

with a decreasing discount rate, in other words less impulsiveness or income and the magnitude of rewards.[17]

Discounting is only one of the many problems that plague *commitment* situations, in which our cooperative behavior is justified only if other people engage in equally cooperative behavior, and there is no easy way to predict or enforce cooperation. For instance, marriage requires a significant investment of resources (emotional, material) and some opportunity costs that cannot be recouped unless the other partner invests in a similar manner. An employer counts on a prospective employee's honesty and willingness to work, many aspects of which are non-enforceable. Soldiers in a platoon need to be sure that their comrades will risk their lives for them if necessary – and it will be too late to punish them if they don't. Commitment situations require commitment devices that make cooperation more likely. In some communities abandoning one's spouse brings about such a cost in reputation that marriage vows are credible. Soldiers and sportsmen test their partners through hazing to gain some idea of their "mettle".[18]

For cooperation to work out, one should be able to persuade others that one will not defect. It is generally not sufficient to declare one's willingness to cooperate – for that kind of promise is among the weapon of cheaters. One needs to credible commitment signals. For instance, a suitor who evinces a mild form of romantic madness seems more credible than a one who describes his feelings as quite rational. An employee who seems naturally honest may stand more of a chance of being hired than one who coldly reflects on the costs and dangers of theft. In many cases, commitment signals consist in tying one's own hands to avoid behaving in an opportunistic manner. A famous example is Ulysses asking his companions to tie him to the mast lest he dive to join the sirens. In business, many trade associations work as similar devices, as they ostracize or even sue those members that misbehave; so those who join the association are in effect tying their own hands, depriving themselves of the opportunity to defraud customers.[19]

Decision-makers could be pulled away from these impulsive courses of action if considering them triggered a negative reward – equal to or greater than the imminent one. Now that is precisely what moral emotions seem to provide. Considering impulsive actions like mugging and forgetting about musical practice makes (many of) us ashamed of ourselves – a negative reward that seems to overshadow whatever benefit we could get from pursuing these courses of action. Conversely, positive emotions like pride provide us with

---

17 GREEN/MYERSON, *A discounting framework for choice with delayed and probabilistic rewards* [2004], 772–777.

18 See DE ALBUQUERQUE/PAES-MACHADO, *The hazing machine* [2004]; SCHNUR, *Fraternity Hazing* [2008].

19 ELSTER, *Ulysses and the Sirens* [1979], 103–111; FRANK, *Passions within Reason* [1988]; SCHELLING, *The Strategy of Conflict* [1960].

immediate positive rewards when we engage in immediately costly behaviors like protecting old ladies or donating some of our income.

More generally, one can describe a class of strategic incentives (embodied in feelings, cognitions, and institutions) with the following features:

(1) They sway us towards cooperative strategies, away from opportunistic, impulsive, immediately beneficial behaviors.
(2) They do so by providing immediate rewards that counter the effects of discounting.
(3) Their appearance and their gradual increase in importance are sufficiently advantageous to the individual to survive evolution by natural selection.
(4) They are uncontrolled in the sense that they are not, or not greatly, influenced by the subject's current goals. As we saw above, many commitment devices consist in tying our own hands, so we cannot any longer act on our goals (we cannot leave the ship and follow the sirens). In the same way, moral feelings direct our behavior only to the extent that we cannot help but feel them.

Cooperation often requires that people sacrifice an immediate benefit for a delayed reward, an arrangement that goes against the grain of evolved discounting strategies. A possible solution is to evolve a system of emotions that provide immediate negative rewards (e.g. guilt) for opportunistic behaviors and positive ones (e.g. pride) for cooperation. However, these dispositions are worthwhile only if they (1) override rational self-interest, and (2) are honestly signaled. This may be why some emotions and moral feelings associated with cooperation are neither rational nor easy to conceal. According to Robert Frank, they constitute commitment devices whereby one ties one's own hands in order to signal a disposition to cooperate, thereby garnering the benefit of being seen as a reliable partner.[20]

Some human preferences may have evolved because they constituted such commitment devices and allowed long-term cooperation, among them moral feelings. Robert Frank argues that such feelings as pride, guilt, spite and mercy are necessary to non-opportunistic behavior, as they provide a specific reward, either positive (pride, gratitude) or negative (guilt, shame, moral disgust). As we consider prospective courses of action, the non-prosocial ones (mug the old lady, don't give to charity) are attractive because of the discount rate that diminishes the value of expected distant outcomes, either negative or positive (do time in jail, be seen as selfish). By contrast, the payoff is immediate (get or save the money) and therefore triggers the anticipation of imminent positive reward.[21] Also, this would explain why a central moral emotion is outrage, typically caused by moral violations that result in denial of one's

20 See FRANK, *Passions within Reason* [1988].
21 FRANK, *Cooperation through emotional commitment* [2001], 65.

share in normal cooperation. A crucial cognitive capacity in exchange is cheater-detection and a crucial motivation is the desire to punish cheaters.[22]

Different kinds of evidence converge to suggest that moral dispositions are indeed commitment devices. People's typical behavior in economic experiments, in real markets, in social-psychological protocols, are best explained in terms of uncontrollable, non-opportunistic emotional systems, the outcome of which is visible to others and therefore constitutes an adequate signaling system. Also relevant to this picture is the appearance of moral judgment and feelings in children. As we said above, on evolutionary grounds it seems difficult to understand that morality is simply rammed down young children's throats. Indeed, developmental evidence shows that young children have an early understanding of moral imperatives. In particular, even pre-schoolers judge that moral norms, especially concerning justice or harm to others, are compelling whether or not they are expressed by an authority, apply to all places and contexts, and justify punishment when violated.[23] These intuitions are remarkably stable across cultures. Moral understandings, far from being dependent upon socially transmitted conceptual frames, develop before such concepts are intelligible to children, and regardless of what religious concepts are entertained by adults around the child (indeed, regardless of whether there are any religious concepts in the child's cultural environment). Interestingly, many early-developing and strongly emotional norms focus on (1) social coordination (e.g. norms about sharing, cooperating, not harming others) and (2) coalitional signals (e.g. norms about etiquette, disgust at strangers' typical behaviors). This is why it makes sense to describe the development of moral feelings and intuitions in the context of evolved dispositions for social interaction.

Could "religion" be a form of prosocial signaling?

Recently, a number of authors have proposed that religious thought and behavior may be involved in the appearance of prosocial behaviors in humankind.[24] These authors do not make the ancient mistake of assuming that religious doctrines are the source of moral intuitions. Their model is based on evolutionary reasoning. Specifically, the first point is that religious activities in most human societies seem unmotivated and costly. Given that sacrificing to the ancestors provides no advantage whatever, and therefore has no fitness

22 PRICE/COSMIDES/TOOBY, *Punitive sentiment as an anti-free rider psychological device* [2002], 214–217.

23 See TURIEL, *The Development of Social Knowledge* [1983].

24 See BULBULIA, *Religious costs as adaptions that signal altruistic intention* [2004]; IRONS, *Religion as a hard-to-fake sign of commitment* [2002]; SOSIS, *Religion and intragroup cooperation* [2000].

impact, why would people, the world over, be compelled to engage in such behaviors? The cost of religious behavior consists in expensive activities like performing extravagant ceremonies, building shrines or monuments, wasting time in communal rituals. As one author has noted, "most religions are expressed in elaborate rituals that are costly in time and sometimes in other ways."[25] Initiation rites are generally painful, and many rites require expensive preparations. In a more general way, religious thought and behavior would seem to mobilize cognitive resources away from survival and reproduction, and focus them on imagined agents of no importance for fitness.

Now this situation is not unfamiliar to evolutionary biologists, who for some time have had to explain the occurrence of costly, apparently maladaptive behaviors in many species. For instance, some gazelles jump high when they detect predators, at the cost of attracting their attention, and peacocks grow enormous trains that constitute an enormous drag on their energy and also make them vulnerable to predators. Under what circumstances could such behaviors have evolved? This is less of a mystery if we construe them as a form of signal – which conveys, in the gazelle's case, that it is nimble enough to escape predators and therefore probably not worth the lion's effort. In Zahavi's term, these signals follow the "handicap principle". By handicapping yourself, you demonstrate that you have enough resources to escape predators.[26] Handicaps are one among the many forms of what biologists call "honest" signals – which accurately convey the state of the individual emitting the signal, because they would be very costly to fake. That is, a peacock that did not have the strength to escape predators *and* carry his tail would be too vulnerable – so the tail is an index of great reserves in available resources.

Signals are especially important in an intensely social species like humans, who can be said to live in the "cognitive niche", that is, to survive on information extracted from the natural and social environment. Information about conspecifics is crucial to social exchange, especially information about their intentions and dispositions, because there are clear and immediate rewards for opportunistic defection, that is, for reaping the benefits of social exchange without paying its costs. Signals about commitment are, obviously, crucial to social interaction.

Some evolutionary anthropologists see religious behavior as such a form of honest signaling. In this case, rather than conveying messages about physical fitness, individuals signal their social dispositions, which are of course crucial to other humans. Commitment to a religious group comes at a cost, as we said above. In places where many different religious affiliations compete, it also has the additional opportunity cost, that by joining a particular congregation,

25 IRONS, *Religion as a hard-to-fake sign of commitment* [2002], 293.
26 ZAHAVI/ZAHAVI, *The Handicap Principle* [1997], 24.

people exclude themselves from all the other groups. Can we interpret all this in terms of signaling?

The model is plausible in that religious affiliation is generally public and of great interest to other people. A great deal of religious activity is both public and formalized, so that people's commitment to the local ritual system is observable by all. Also, people in many societies seem exceedingly interested in other individuals' religious thoughts, which on the face of it would seem odd. Why should it matter to us, what other people think about superhuman agents or how they interact with such agents? In particular, why should it be so important to many people that others have the *same* metaphysical thoughts? The signaling model would account for these features in a parsimonious way. What matters in people's public adherence to this or that metaphysics is of course not the metaphysics itself, but the willingness to incur costs for gaining membership in the group.

There is also some empirical evidence to support this model. Explaining commitment as signal would predict that religious groups that make the price of entry (or the price of remaining) in the group higher would be more strongly integrated, with less dissension or defection. On the basis of a comparative study of small communities, Sosis showed that cost is indeed an important factor. Religious groups that require a greater investment in costly rituals tend to remain more cohesive.[27] This framework requires a significant change of perspective in our understanding of religious activity. First, it describes religion mostly in terms of communication rather than internal beliefs. What matters here is what people demonstrate to others. Second, it suggests that internal states, beliefs, and emotions may be tools recruited in the development of such demonstrations.

All this may be valid, but the model is less than altogether compelling, as things stand, for several reasons. For one thing, the costly signal hypothesis suggests that religion is a straightforward adaptation. Dispositions to entertain religious thoughts and communicate them to others emerged because of their impact on fitness.[28] Obviously, such a strong claim requires equally strong empirical evidence, which in turn depends on more precise hypotheses. One must specify to what extent "religion" is actually costly and signaling, in the precise sense required by biological models.[29] Also, the framework implies that costly behaviors are the original ones, and non-costly ones a by-product. This might imply psychological predictions, e. g. as to the relative impact of costly vs. non-costly practices on receiver psychology, on the mental states of potential believers. In other words, these models perhaps

---

27 Sosis, *Why aren't we all hutterites?* [2003], 115 f; Sosis/Bressler, *Cooperation and communue longevity* [2003].

28 See Bulbulia, *Religious costs as adaptions that signal altruistic intention* [2004].

29 See Cronk, *Evolutionary theories of morality and the manipulative use of signals* [1994].

need to be supplemented with the psychological proximate causation that is currently missing.

More important, there is a great ambiguity in the way proponents of this model describe what they call "religion". That ambiguity is unfortunately typical of discussions of religion and evolution. It consists in focusing on particular traits of religious behaviors and institutions and making them a universal feature of human behavior, when they are most likely a recent by-product of social evolution. This is very much the case when we describe religious behavior in the form of membership of different, competing institutions. As I explained in chapter 1, the anthropological and historical evidence suggests that for most of their evolutionary history, humans did not have religions in that sense. The environment that shaped human dispositions is that of very small groups, perhaps with all sorts of supernatural notions and beliefs in superhuman agents, but certainly not with organized groups of religious specialists, or competing religious affiliations.

The argument that religious behavior could create prosocial behavior, via costly commitment with a signaling function, seems to be based on a misunderstanding of the evolution of religious concepts and norms. It maybe the case – I very much doubt the validity of a very restrictive set of studies in this case, but let us grant this for the sake of argument – it may be the case that membership in particular religious institutions, in some countries, strength-ens some forms of prosocial behavior. It is therefore tempting to see "religion" as one of the possible factors in the development of human strong reciprocity and prosocial behavior.

But "religion" in the form examined in these studies is a recent invention, so recent in fact (a few millennia) and initially so restricted in space, that it could hardly have had any effect on the common genetic makeup of humankind. What people have had for a long time, and certainly in those ancestral periods that shaped our modern genotypes, is a collection of religious thoughts and behaviors that do *not* resemble the modern institutionalized form in any sense. Overwhelming ethnographic and archaeological evidence shows that people throughout those periods engaged in non-doctrinal religious activities, with no full-time religious priests, no clear doctrine, no notion of "our religion", no need for standardized rituals. So the notion of religion as a prosocial adaptation tries to explain a stable feature of human minds (a disposition for religious thoughts and behaviors) in terms of a very recent historical accident (competitive, doctrinal religious institutions) with no evolutionary impact.

Given this background, it would make sense to assume that humans evolved all sorts of ways to demonstrate their commitment to their social groups – but religious commitment would not be one of them, since there were no doctrines to commit oneself to, no large scale ceremonies to invest in. So, evolutionary biology and archaeology would suggest that the "religion as costly signaling" model is less than parsimonious. People do invent commitment signals – that much is true, and made obvious by hundreds of observations and experiments. When their social environment includes notions of competing religious affiliation, they can of course use these as commitment signals – but competing religious affiliations are not a stable feature of human evolutionary history.

So why are superhuman agents also moral enforcers?

Despite the difficulties of some current models, it does make sense to wonder about the evolutionary background of various religious dispositions, among them the widespread association between superhuman agents and practical moral issues. In most human cultures, most people consider that some superhuman agents have something at stake in their own decision-making. They assume that ancestors, gods or other such agents (at least sometimes) care about what humans do, and certainly can perceive it. I called this the "interested party" notion of superhuman agency, the idea that, inasmuch as some action has some moral component, gods and ancestors know about it and may react to it.[30] This stands in contrast to the kinds of religious morality commonly offered by religious guilds, such as religious codes (moral behavior is construed as adherence to a set of rules provided by the institution), and moral exemplars (moral behavior is then construed as emulation of particular individuals – Gautama, Muhammad, etc). These last two forms of religious morality are a recent invention of religious guilds, but the interested party model seems to be the major mode in which people (even in institutionalized religious communities) think of morality and superhuman agency. We find it in many world religions, whether or not theologians find it acceptable. Most Christians entertain this notion that every single one of their moral choices is relevant to their personal connection to God. That is, God not only gave laws and principles, but also pays attention to what people do. For obvious reasons, the notion that supernatural agents are interested parties is generally associated with the idea that the gods or spirits are powerful and that it is within their capacities to inflict all sorts of calamities upon people – or help them prosper – depending on their behavior.

Religious morality is the combination of this notion of interested agent – superhuman agents who have a stake in what we do – and the human propensity, described in chapter 2, to engage in sustained social relations with absent or imagined agents. It therefore does not really differ from standard morality, of the non-religious kind, the kind of moral intuition, emotion and reasoning that occurs without reference to superhuman agency. Indeed, the scientific study of moral cognition seems to reverse the standard view of the

30 See BOYER, *Functional origins of religious concepts* [2000].

connections between religions and morality, described at the beginning of this chapter. It is not really plausible that religions are the sole providers of moral values. As we said, morality existed long before religions, and in most places on earth has no connection with religious thoughts. But we can go further – religions inasmuch as they promote some moral codes or prescriptions, are actually dependent on non-religious moral sentiment and implicit principles. Religious morality is parasitic upon spontaneous morality, attempts to reframe it in metaphysical terms, but it does not change or expand the evolved cognitive processes on which this spontaneous morality is based.

In a series of experiments with children and adults, Jesse Bering has demonstrated that subjects readily consider non-physical or dead agents as participants in their current situation. Children and adults are prepared to entertain the notion that non-physical agents are trying to communicate with them, and – importantly – these agents are generally (though implicitly) construed as having full access to morally relevant aspects of a situation, such as people's motivations and the moral value of their actions. Supernatural agents thereby come to be involved in representing how our actions would seem to others – particularly in terms of moral judgment.[31]

Epilogue

Most students of religion take for granted that religiously coded morality must have an effect on people's moral intuitions. I have yet to come across any actual evidence for this effect. True, people's explicit discourse, whereby they justify the intuitions, is certainly affected by local religious concepts. But that kind of discourse is *a posteriori.* We have no evidence that it modifies the intuitions themselves. On the contrary, cross-cultural evidence shows a great convergence in moral intuitions despite great differences both in explicit moral codes and in supernatural beliefs.

Religious concepts do not change people's moral intuitions but frame these intuitions in terms that make them easier to think about. For instance, in most human groups supernatural agents are thought to be interested parties in people's interactions. Given this assumption, having the intuition that an action is wrong becomes having the expectation that a personalized agent disapproves of it. The social consequences of the latter way of representing the situation are much clearer to the agent, as they are handled by specialized mental systems for social interaction. This notion of gods and spirits as interested parties is far more salient in people's moral inferences than the notion of these agents as moral legislators or moral exemplars.

---

31 See Boyer, *Religion Explained* [2001].

4. Is there a religious experience?

Religious phenomena do not only consist of thoughts and beliefs and norms but also of specific behaviors. This leads many people to think that what religions bring people is a specific kind of experience, and that understanding what this kind of experience is or what brings it about, or what it does to people, is important to understanding the spread of religious notions. Indeed, it is sometimes argued that experience is the foundation of religiosity – and concepts and norms are nothing without that specific quality of experience. I think this argument is misguided, and that a scientific consideration of religious behaviors can show us why. Obviously, the question is not whether people who perform religious acts are having a particular experience – they are, just like they are when they eat carrots or play the piano. Every mental activity is a special kind of experience, with a particular feel that we can recognize. No, the question is whether there is a specifically religious kind of experience, with features common to different religious behaviors, and not usually found, or not in the same way, in non-religious contexts. That is less than certain – indeed I will argue that there is probably no such thing as religious experience in this specific sense.

Why bother with experience?

What is the role of exceptional experience in the acquisition and transmission of religious concepts and behaviors? This is an old theme in the study of religion, one which William James saw as foundational: people having such experiences becoming inspired leaders or prophets.[1] Also, experience might be seen as a powerful factor in the diffusion of religious belief, to the extent that it provides undeniable subjective grounding to concepts and norms acquired from other people. Diverse attempts have been made to relate evolutionary history and prehistory to a disposition for religious experience.[2] However, one must first be specific about the range of "experience" considered relevant. The anthropological or psychological understanding of the term includes such phenomena as trance, possession, and the feeling of a supernatural presence.[3]

---

1 JAMES, *The Varieties of Religious Experience* [1902], 334–339.
2 PROUDFOOT, *Religious Experience* [1985], 190–227.
3 See ARGYLE, *The psychological explanation of religious experience* 1990; BOYATZIS, *A critique of models of religious experience* [2001]; PROUDFOOT, *Religious Experience* [1985].

In the field of religious studies, Caroline Davis proposed the following list of phenomena usually mentioned in this context: (1) interpretive experiences: events, such as fortuitous co-incidences, that are interpreted in religious terms; (2) quasi-sensory experiences, visions, voices, dreams, etc; (3) revelatory experiences, sudden moments of insight; (4) regenerative experiences – profound feelings of strength, comfort or joy; (5) numinous experiences – feeling insignificant in the presence of gods; (6) mystical experiences – feelings of oneness, serenity and a loss of the sense of space and time.[4] More generally, the literature on religious experience focuses on such features as loss of control, positive valence, feelings of benevolence and compassion, as well as the impression of presence of superhuman agents.[5]

The occurrence of such mental states is beyond doubt, but do they matter? I ask the question bluntly because in most debates on the question it has been taken for granted (1) that such experiences are *sui generis*, that is, special to "religion"; and (2) that they are crucial to understanding religious thoughts, their emergence and development in humankind – at any rate more so than standard, humdrum thoughts and behaviors directed at superhuman agents. To me it is quite clear that both assumptions are false, that the form of experience described is not unique to religious contexts; and that it is virtually irrelevant in explaining the evolution of religious cognitions.

The feelings mentioned by Davis (loss of control, positive feelings, impression that one has reached above or beyond normal existence) are found in combination in a great many forms of human experience (from mountaineering to recreational drug-taking and from frantic music-making to accidental hyperventilation). Since that much is obvious, it would seem futile to even consider "religious experience" as a special form of experience – it is no more special than "mountaineering experience". It is very difficult to argue that what is described as religious experience forms a natural kind, distinct from other states of consciousness (e. g. those experienced by non-religious individuals).[6] This is confirmed by comparative studies, in that disciplines of meditation and trance can support diametrical interpretations, for instance in terms of powerful agency (Sufism) or in terms of agency as an illusion (Lamaism). So why would many scholars devote so much energy to this question?

The question naturally leads to the second premise, that a particular form of experience is essential to the emergence of persistence of religious thoughts. In the history of religious scholarship, this notion has taken several forms, either normative or descriptive. What I would call the normative version of the

---

4 See Davis, *The Evidential Force of Religious Experience* [1989]. Cited and discussed by Sharf, *Experience* [1989].

5 See Moehle, *Cognitive Dimensions of religious experiences* [1983].

6 See Pyysiäinen, *Magic, Miracles, and Religion* [2004]; Ratcliffe, *Neurotheology: A Science of What?* [2006].

"experience-based religion" attitude is the assumption that special mental states matter, even if they do not actually have much influence on most people's religious thoughts, because they constitute a "truer" or "deeper" version of religion. In that view, everyday rituals and prayers are a superficial or unimportant way of connecting to superhuman agency. One gains a greater understanding of superhuman agency by some form of direct experience. I will not discuss this particular version, as it obviously falls outside the scope of natural science.

More interesting, the descriptive version was offered for instance by William James, suggesting a recurrent script for the development of religious traditions. Inspired leaders or mediums, on the basis of exceptional experience, would put forth religious thoughts that the populace, without the benefit of exceptional mental events, would turn into religious traditions.[7] Here experience does matter because the conceptual content of religious traditions only makes sense in view of its original experiential context. The problem with this version was simply that most historical and anthropological evidence suggests the opposite causal route – that inspired individuals are heard only to the extent that their message is relevant, given people's prior concepts, and that the new message generally has little if any impact on people's actual thoughts and behaviors. Despite its intuitive plausibility, this quasi-Weberian scenario (inspired charismatic leaders fostering innovations that are then routinized by the populace) is not altogether accurate.[8] As I remarked in chapter 2, widespread explicit doctrinal statements only have a marginal effect on implicit religious assumptions. Even when whole churches and traditions are based on the innovations of some inspired leader, this does not entail that people's thoughts have been durably transformed.

If we want to understand the emergence and recurrence of religious thoughts and behaviors, it seems more important to focus on these phenomena themselves, rather than some exceptional states, which only occur rarely, among only a few people, and seem to have little if any influence on the phenomenon we proposed to study. If I may at this point venture a personal opinion, I would suspect that many people's apparent interest in the descriptive claims (religion did start from exceptional experiences) is mostly motivated by their adherence to the normative one (there is some deeper truth to be found in special experience than in ordinary religious cognition).

7 JAMES, *The Varieties of Religious Experience* [1902], 334–339.
8 WEBER, *Wirtschaft und Gesellschaft* [1956], 669 ff.

Who invented "religious experience"?

Religious experience is not a natural kind. There are few important features that can be found in the different forms of special experience associated with religious content, and all of these features can be found in non-religious contexts. So why has the concept any currency? In a serious and important sense, the notion was invented. That is, some scholars stipulated that one could isolate *those* special mental states that did occur in religious contexts. How did that happen?

At this point, one may suspect that I am being either eccentric or ignorant. After all, do we not all know that experience, as opposed to discourse or doctrine, is fundamental to many non-Western traditions? By insisting that we should focus on people's mental representations, as opposed to non-verbal, possibly non-conceptual mental states, is one not biased by the Western habit of making discourse central to human life? I would say that, on the contrary, it is the insistence on experience that is ethnocentric. Far from being central, specific experience is either unimportant or completely irrelevant to most people's religious activity in most cultures.

Let me start with tribal societies and their "traditional" religious behaviors. Religious notions and norms in such groups do include specifications for rituals to perform and how to perform them but there is rarely any emphasis on or indeed even mention of the special quality of conscious experience that may accompany these rituals. Indeed, in most traditional systems of this kind no-one seems to show any interest whatever in how people "feel" about ancestors, gods and spirits. Questions about such inner states would strike most people as totally irrelevant to the business at hand, in the same way as it would seem strange to wonder whether your lodger pays her rent with feigned or sincere conviction – what matters is that she does pay. This is a very general feature of most non-scholarly religious traditions. One reason why these religious traditions may seem to trigger and require particular experiences is that they invariably require ritualized behavior – and doesn't such behavior correspond to highly specific states? I will return to that question presently. For the moment, let me emphasize again that talk about experience is largely absent from most non-literate religious contexts.

What about non-Western, literate "world" religions? This is the domain where most people would see a crucial role for special experience. The fascination for experience is often projected to the "East", a conflation of Indian, Chinese and other "oriental" religions, supposedly at the antipodes of a modern, and Western insistence on doctrine, deduction and conformity. This impression derives most of its appeal from popular images of Buddhism based on meditation and other such mental disciplines, of Hinduism and its ascetics, of Islam and the Sufi ecstatic ceremonies.

However, as Robert Sharf has shown, a closer inspection of these traditions suggests that the contrast is misleading – and that a supposed emphasis on experience is mostly the product of a distorted Western perception of these traditions.[9] The distortion results first and foremost from a systematic bias in Western scholarship, a decision to focus for instance on the mystical aspects of Japanese and Tibetan Buddhism, to the detriment of the many non-mystical trends in these traditions. In practice, this has meant that practices that were often marginal in their original contexts have been taken as central by Western students of religion. Given this bias, only few people have paid attention to the fact that, e.g. meditation or other practices were, if admitted, generally construed as convenient tools, including pedagogical tools, rather than central elements of the tradition. Indeed, Sharf also demonstrates that, ironically, most Japanese and Indian statements about the preeminence of experience over doctrine were actually crucially influenced by Western philosophy of religion and phenomenology.[10] This is the case, and a historically documented case, for such apologists Radhakrishnan for Hinduism and Suzuki for Zen Buddhism. Both took their inspiration for an "Eastern" view of religion from William James and various other Western philosophers of religion. Far from being a product of local, immemorial religious traditions, the emphasis on experience was a local, modern and reformist adaptation of recent Western philosophy.

Monks and magnets

Another way in which experience is salient in modern discourse on religious behavior is the great vogue of studies of "religion and the brain", in particular of neuro-imaging studies. The point of these is to find out what neural structures are activated when people engage in specifically religious activities. Such studies imply that there is actually some specific form of conscious experience that can be found in prayer, meditation or visions, that is absent from non-religious contexts. Indeed, these studies require this assumption, because otherwise there would not be anything to study.

Neuro-imaging, at least in its first phase, led to an extraordinary development in studies of "the neural correlates of x", in which x may be anything from the highly reasonable (episodic memory, attention shifts, reasoning, etc) to anything that could catch the attention of a larger public (love, fashion accessories, soap operas, etc).[11] It is not always easy to sort the wheat from the chaff, but a rule of thumb is that neuro-imaging studies make sense to the extent that (1) the x in question is fairly clearly defined, (2) there are precise hypotheses about its psychological properties, that is, how the

---

9 See SHARF, *Experience* [1998].
10 See SHARF, *Experience* [1998].
11 See RAICHLE, *Modern phrenology* [1999].

process in question could be implemented in a computational organ, and (3) there are also hypotheses that can be confirmed or disconfirmed by finding out exactly which neural structures are actually involved in x. To take a simple example, it made great sense to explore the "neural correlates of face-recognition", because (1) the phenomenon was clearly defined (face-perception is different from the rest of visual perception, indeed some patients can be impaired in face-recognition and not in other visual capacities); (2) there were clear hypotheses that face-perception consisted in two distinct sub-processes, for the details and for the global perception of the face respectively; (3) these hypotheses were confirmed by the specific activation of a temporal gyrus in face-perception as opposed to other visual stimuli.[12]

It would be optimistic to say that the situation is similar for the "neural correlates of religious experience". Indeed, the first problem is that, as I mentioned above, no-one has a precise understanding of what they mean by religious experience, or indeed definite evidence that such a thing exists. Besides, none of the religion scholars interested in "experience" seems to have any precise psychological model of that putative form of experience. Although a number of recent studies have documented the specific neural correlates of meditation and trance, these states do not require concepts of non-physical agency – indeed they do not seem to require any precise conceptual content.[13] In the long run, such studies may well tell us all sorts of interesting things about brain function – but they are unlikely to tell us much about the mythical object "religious experience".

So, again, it may be interesting to understand why these kinds of studies exert such fascination. To start with, there seems to be a great appeal to the notion of visualizing experience – even more so when the experience in question is slightly mysterious (deep meditation) and attractive to modern audiences (Buddhist monks). But all this seems baffling to most cognitive psychologists or neuroscientists. After all, *any* experience corresponds to specific neural activation, and therefore could be visualized in terms of cortical areas that "light up" in a scanner, so why focus on that particular one? That is all the more relevant as the experience in question, as I said above, is defined in the most nebulous terms.

The attractiveness of such studies may stem from the (fundamentally misguided) notion that they tell us something about the "truth" or "reality" of mystical and other religious experience. Indeed, the rhetoric of many popular accounts of these findings strongly supports that interpretation.[14] Research into neural activation is presented as addressing the fundamental question,

---

12 See KANWISHER, *Domain specificity in face perception* [2000].
13 AZARI et al., *Neural correlates of religious experience* [2001], 1649 – 1652; PERSINGER, *Near death experiences and ecstasy* [1999].
14 See NEWBERG/D'AQUILI, *The neuropsychology of spiritual experience* [1998].

whether mystical and other non-standard "religious" experience is "real". But note that this is deeply – I would say criminally – ambiguous. To say that an experience is real may mean two very different things: either that the experience really took place (you are not lying or joking, when you say you saw an elephant in the hall) or that it is about something real (there was an elephant in the hall). Neural studies can only, to some extent, address the first question; people who claim to have visions or to enter deep stages of meditation are actually in some mental state that is different from ordinary experience, and this is reflected in specific neural activation. Obviously, neuro-imaging cannot address the second question, whether for instance visions are actual perceptions of something real, but that is certainly the question that attracts a wide readership. Neuro-imaging of religion may derive most of its appeal from this (perhaps not deliberate) bait-and-switch, from a fascinating but intractable question to a solvable but unimportant one.

Rituals: a real (and most common) form of religious experience

In all these disquisitions on religious experience, the main concern is on personal and often individual practices and traditions. But a much more widespread form of "religious experience" is the participation in religious rituals. This would seem a much more promising path for understanding the role of experience, if any, in the emergence and diffusion of religious thoughts and behaviors. Ritual is relatively neglected in studies of religious "experience", which may well reflect the anti-ritualist bias of some modern religions.[15] But that is hardly justified from a scientific viewpoint. After all, ritual performances are widespread, indeed quasi-universal, they are associated in many contexts with religious thoughts, and they may well correspond to a specific form of experience. So what occurs during rituals, and what is the connection with religious concepts and norms?

This question is made much more complicated than it should be by the fact that there is no agreed definition of ritual, and no clear criterion by which cultural anthropologists or other scholars of religion or classics determine that a particular type of behavior is or is not an instance of a ritual. "Ritual," like "marriage" or "religion," is not a proper analytical category. It seems to be largely based on a family resemblance between instances.[16] That is why it is certainly futile to collect many instances of what are commonly called "rituals" and to tabulate their common features. This too often results in very vague formulations that would potentially apply to any social institution.

Classical anthropology and psychology of religion assumed that rituals

15 Douglas, *Natural Symbols* [1982], 1–18.
16 See Needham, *Polyethic classification: convergence and consequences* [1975].

made it possible to convey deep symbolic meanings. This view seems less than compelling to cognitive anthropologists, given that many rituals include vague, incoherent, paradoxical, or just plain meaningless elements.[17] Indeed, ritualization reduces rather than increases the amount of information potentially conveyed.[18] So why should there be a disposition for such behaviors?

Pierre Lienard and I tried to make sense of a subset of rituals, the kind of performance that we called "ritualized behavior", which may or may not be found in any particular instance of what are commonly called rituals.[19] Ritualized behavior is a specific way of organizing the flow of behavior, characterized by compulsion (one must perform the particular sequence), rigidity (it must be performed the right way), redundancy (the same actions are often repeated inside the ritual), and goal demotion (the actions are divorced from their usual goals). Although ritualized behavior in this precise sense is typically the hallmark of ceremonies we call "rituals," it certainly is not found in all of those. Conversely, there may be many contexts outside "rituals" that include ritualized behavior.

Although "ritual" is a nebulous term, ritualized behavior is not. One can identify it in terms of specific features:

No obvious empirical goals. In rituals one typically washes instruments that are already clean, one enters rooms to exit them straightaway, one talks to interlocutors that are manifestly absent, and so forth. Many rituals include actions for which there could not possibly be any clear empirical goal, such as rubbing an animal's forehead with one's body, passing a chicken from hand to hand in a circle, or going round a temple several times. True, a given ritual generally has a specific purpose (e.g., healing a particular person) but the set of sequences that compose the ritual are generally not connected to this goal in any explicit or meaningful manner. People feel that they should perform the ritual in the exact way prescribed and generally in the way it was performed on previous occasions. (This obviously does not mean that ceremonies are actually performed in the same way. What is important is that people strive to achieve a performance that matches their representation of past performances, and that they attach great emotional weight to any deviation from that remembered pattern).[20]

Repetition and redundancy. Repeated enactments of the same action or gesture – as well as reiterations of the same utterances – are typical of many collective rituals. People bow or kneel repeatedly; they walk around an animal seven times, which clearly signals that no effect is achieved by any specific

---

17 See HUMPHREY/LAIDLAW, *Archetypal Actions* [1993]; see STAAL, *Rules without Meaning* [1990].
18 BLOCH, *Symbols, song, dance, and features of articulation* [1974], 76 f.
19 See BOYER/LIENARD, *Why ritualized behaviour in humans?* [2006]; LIENARD/BOYER, *Whence Collective Rituals* [2006].
20 See BOYER, *Tradition as Truth and Communication* [1990].

iteration of the action. A given sequence is executed three or five or ten times. What matters is the exact number. What matters too is that the action should seem identical in all these iterations. This makes many ritual sequences clearly distinct from everyday action, in which there is either no repetition of identical sequences (e. g., in assembling a musical instrument, one performs a series of unique actions), or each repeated sequence has a specific outcome (in weaving, the warp is changed at each step), or repetition is cumulative (the egg whites rise only after a long period of stirring).

Order and boundaries. In many rituals, people create an orderly environment that is quite different from the one of everyday interaction. People line up instead of walking, they dance instead of moving, they wear special clothes or makeup, they build alignments of rocks or logs, they create elaborate color and shape combinations, and so forth. There is a lot of ordering in rituals that is quite distinct from the comparatively unpredictable patterns of non-ritual environments. Related to this is the recurrent concern with delimiting a particular space (a "sacred" circle, a taboo territory). People emphasize the boundary between this space and the rest, for instance by special prohibitions (only men enter the sacred circle, only women sit on the left side, etc.) or by restrictions on communication between marked and unmarked spaces.

Purity and danger. Pollution and cleansing, protection against invisible dangers, and the creation of a special space and time are common themes associated with ritualized behavior. In many rituals, blood, semen, or excrement are a primary concern, the miasma or smells of decaying corpses are important, and the use of water or fire as possible ways of getting rid of pollution and contaminants is also recurrent. There are also innumerable examples of allusions to purity and pollution in ritual requirements. People must wash before prayers, they immerse themselves in water to rid themselves of pollution, they must wear spotless garments, the sacrificial animal must be absolutely clean, menstruating women (supposedly polluted and polluting) are barred from rituals spaces, and so on. This concern with pollution and cleansing is so prevalent that it has been considered a foundation of religious ritual.[21]

Why do we find these features together? In any particular case of ritualized behavior, we could try to elicit diverse conceptual associations that link the particular actions to underlying or implicit cultural models. That is what cultural anthropologists do – and it is certainly crucial to making sense of particular ceremonies, but it does not address the general question, why ritualized behavior occurs at all, and why it combines these particular features, in so many different cultural contexts.

---

21 DOUGLAS, *Purity and Danger* [1966], 8 – 35, *Natural symbols* [1982], 105.

Ritualized behavior and precaution systems

As Lienard and I emphasized, ritualized behavior is by no means specific to religious or indeed other kinds of collective ceremonies. It is also a hallmark in most human cultures of children's behavior during early childhood, and characteristic of a specific pathology, obsessive-compulsive disorder (hereafter: OCD).

Most children engage in ritualistic behaviors at a particular stage of development, starting at age two, peaking at age five, and subsiding around age seven. The age of onset is similar in different cultures, as are the themes of ritualistic behavior: perfectionism, attachment to favorite objects, concerns about dirt and cleanliness, preoccupation with just-right ordering of objects, preferred household routines.[22]

In some people, intrusive thoughts and compulsions can evolve into full-blown obsessive-compulsive disorder. The main feature of the pathology is a strong compulsion to engage in stereotyped and repetitive activities with no rational justification. Some patients engage in bouts of washing or cleaning tools or utensils. Others verify that they locked their door, rolled up the car window, or turned off the gas knobs over and over again. In most cases the ritual seems to be an intuitive response to obsessive thoughts about potential danger, notably contamination and contagion (e.g., fear to catch other people's germs, to ingest contaminated substances, to pass on diseases to one's children or others), possible harm to others or to oneself (e.g., handling kitchen utensils and wounding people), as well as social ostracism following shameful or aggressive acts (thoughts about assaulting others, shouting obscenities, exhibitionism, etc.).

The pathology can be interpreted as a dysfunction (and to a large extent a hyper function) of cognitive systems designed to respond to *potential threats*.[23] On the basis of neurophysiological and neuroimaging evidence, Lienard and I proposed that human minds comprise specialized, evolved vigilance-precaution systems that handle indirect threats to fitness and motivate the organism into taking precautionary behaviors. Most OCD pathology indeed results from dysfunction of the neurocognitive systems dedicated to danger detection and response (basal ganglia) and to planning and inhibition of inappropriate or redundant responses (orbitofrontal cortex in particular). This would explain why the intrusive thoughts of patients are generally focused on a small range of items and concepts connected to

---

22 Zohar/Felz, *Ritualistic behaviour in young children* [2001], 126 f.
23 See Abed/de Pauw, *An evolutionary hypothesis for obsessive compulsory disorder: a psychological immune system* [1998]; Boyer/Lienard, *Why ritualized behaviour in humans?* [2006]; Szechtman/Woody, *Obsessive-compulsive disorder as a disturbance of security motivation* [2004].

recurrent evolutionary threats, such as attack and predation, contagion and contamination, and social threats. It would also explain why the patients rituals seem so often centered on ancient responses to those threats, e. g. washing and cleansing (against pathogens), sustained monitoring and ordering of one's environment (against assault or predation), and excessive monitoring of other people's perception of one's own behavior (to avert social threats).

Children's rituals seem to serve as calibration for these threat-detection and threat-response systems. The rituals focus on dangers of great evolutionary significance and seem to explore possible precautionary behaviors. For instance, children experience the greatest urge to ritualize their environment at the moment of going to sleep, especially if they sleep alone – a situation that is interpreted since infancy as one of great distress and danger. In the same way, young children's spontaneous notions of contagion and contamination, their extreme interest in and reactions to "yucky" stuff, would suggest an exploration of sources of potential danger in their environment. In other words, children are predisposed to entertain notions of potential danger, and approach their environments with certain abstract templates for the description of these dangers. Contamination, for instance, works through invisible vectors.[24] Predation might be expected if one is away from kin, more so at night than during the day.[25] But the specific parameters of potential danger vary greatly according to place and time. That is why the child's precaution systems consist of *learning* rules. Ritualized behaviors are another aspect of this learning process, in which children gradually calibrate their precautionary behaviors as gradually more appropriate responses to potential danger.

What about collective "rituals"?

Many authors, Freud in particular, have commented on the extraordinary similarity between collective (notably religious) ceremonies on the one hand, and individual pathologies like OCD on the other. Comparing hundreds of ritual sequences with clinical descriptions of OCD cases, Fiske and colleagues showed that the same themes recur over and over again in both domains.[26] We would add children's ritualized behaviors as a third manifestation of this puzzling human propensity to organize behavior around highly scripted rites.

However, it is certainly a mistake to construe collective ceremonies as

---

24 ROZIN/MILLMAN/NEMEROFF, *Operation of the laws of sympathetic magic in disgust and other domains* [1986], 709 ff.
25 See BARRETT, *Cognitive development and the understanding of animal behaviour* [2005].
26 DULANEY/FISKE, *Cultural rituals and obsessive-compulsive disorder* [1994], 245, 248; see FREUD, *Zwangshandlungen und Religionsübungen*, 1948 [1906]; RAPOPORT/FISKE, *The new biology of obsessive-compulsive disorder* [1998].

individual pathology writ large, as Freud suggested. In this view, ritual ceremonies were seen as the collective neurosis of a social group. This is misguided because the analogy, is *only* an analogy. Social groups do not have minds or desires or "repression". Even if one admitted Freud's interpretation of what he called the repetition compulsion – which makes no sense in view of our scientific knowledge of OCD – it would still need to be explained how social groups can be affected by such psychodynamic processes. But that is just an aside – we can now see the problem in a different way, on the basis of a better understanding of ritualized behavior.

Before getting into the explanation proper, we must make two important changes to our common assumptions about rituals. First, as I suggested above, there is no such thing as "rituals" as a common category of social phenomena. The term is just too vague, it is not grounded in any recognizable criteria, it does not really denote a natural kind. What we can explain is the occurrence in collective actions of ritualized behavior, which we precisely described above. Many ceremonies that people want to call "rituals" may well include no such behavior. We are only concerned with those that do, and want to explain why they do. Second, ritualization in the sense described so far is quite clearly the opposite of routinization. The latter is a mode of behavior that psychologists would describe as "automaticity". That is, the behavior is controlled by computational processes that do not require conscious attention and cognitive control. For instance, the way most of us tie our shoelaces is automatic or routinized in this sense. Most people can whistle a tune or answer questions or listen to music as they tie their shoelaces. Ritualized behavior as we described it above is exactly the opposite. Having to tie your shoelaces five times with the left hand, then three times with the right hand, without even touching the shoe with your ring finger, implies careful attention and cognitive control of the behavior. One cannot do that and attend to music or conversation or the weather. This contrast between ritualized and routinized behavior is fundamental – the psychological processes are diametrically opposed – yet the term "ritual" includes both, which is yet another reason to abandon it.[27]

Now, why would people assemble and engage in ritualized behavior? Classical anthropological accounts emphasize the possible meanings associated with ceremonies or their social effects. That just begs the question why people would think it appropriate to engage in *ritualized* behavior rather than other kinds of action. The question is perhaps more tractable, if we replace it in the context of a selectionist or epidemiological view of human cultures, which we briefly described in chapter 2. In this framework, there is collective action with ritualized behavior because certain sets of actions are selected through cultural transmission as more "obvious", compelling or natural than other possible sets of actions. We need not assume a specific human need to perform these actions. All we have to assume is that, in given circumstances,

27 See LIENARD/BOYER, *Whence Collective Rituals* [2006].

these sets of actions seem more appropriate than others, certain ritual "recipes" are more attention-grabbing or memorable than others. This selection results in culturally widespread ceremonies.

Our interpretation is that culturally transmitted ritual sequences may be attention-grabbing and compelling to the extent that they implicitly trigger associations with the threat-detection systems described above. As Fiske and others have noted, ritualized ceremonies center on such themes as purity and pollution, cleansing, the invisible vectors of contamination, the imposition of special boundaries and an organized space, hidden danger from unseen, often mystical intruders and enemies.[28] All these themes are such that they activate precaution systems. In computational terms, we would say that such themes provide people with the rationale for performing a particular action, they match the "input format" of threat-detection systems. The kinds of actions performed during such ceremonies also match these input conditions. People are enjoined to wash objects or bodies, to trace limits in space, to monitor their environments, to be mindful of hidden threats.

Culturally transmitted ritualized behavior seems to capture people's attention by mimicking the circumstances of potential threat detection. Such effects of "cognitive capture" are common in human cultures. For instance, people the world over are fascinated by masks because these man-made objects mimic the input conditions of our face-recognition systems.

This suggests that, in order to find ritualized actions compelling, people do not need to be persuaded of the "meanings" conveyed (if any), or be mindful of the social effects of coordinated ceremonies. An action script that does engage our threat-detection systems, or engages them more acutely, is simply more attention-grabbing than one that does not or does it less, and is therefore more likely to be transmitted, thereby becoming a cultural ceremony. Note that this does not in any way imply that people actually think that there is a danger around, no more than people who enjoy masks need think that they are real persons. All that is required is that the relevant cognitive system is activated, which makes the action in question worthy of attention. Over long-term cultural transmission, this would result in apparently compelling, highly prescribed sequences of non-pragmatic actions that often constitute the core of what we call "rituals".

Religion and experience redux

As I noted above, we should be skeptical of claims that religious actions and contexts create a *sui generis* form of conscious experience that could not be found in any other context of human life. However, one type of human

---

28 See Dulaney/Fiske, *Cultural rituals and obsessive-compulsive disorder* [1994].

behavior that we find in many religious contexts, and which does seem to have its special quality, is ritualized behavior. But ritualized behavior is found in many circumstances, which have nothing to do with religious thought and behavior. First, as we saw, ritualized behavior is typical of many children's routines in normal development. Second, there are of course many instances of collective ritualized behavior that have nothing to do with superhuman agency.

For a long time, anthropologists have debated the differences between religious and "secular" rituals, for example, state ceremonies.[29] The distinction does not seem to make much sense, or to be of great use in understanding either form of collective ceremonies. In standard anthropological accounts, religious rituals are the ones in which most participants seem to imagine that some gods or spirits are involved. But this assumption on the part of participants is a statistical phenomenon. Since most forms of collective action, especially when they involve ritualized behavior, are open to multiple interpretations, anyone is free to include gods or spirits in their construal of what they are doing at any specific time. Some participants may well think that the annual Opening of Parliament at Westminster is all about gods, or that a Catholic funeral has nothing to do with superhuman agency. So the notion that the former is a secular, and the latter a religious occasion, is in most instances a *normative* assumption, a claim about what people *should* think, not about what actually happens in their minds. But our aim is to explain what happens, not what should happen, so the distinction between religious and secular is unnecessary.

In many places, people engage in ritualized behavior that they intuitively associate with superhuman agency. Obviously, it is misguided to explain that behavior as a result of having religious thoughts, since human beings can and do engage in ritualized behavior in many other circumstances. The interpretation Lienard and I proposed would suggest that religious notions here are redundant. That is to say, there is a human disposition to perform highly scripted, threat-detection-related sequences of acts, and to be fascinated or at least intrigued by such sequences of actions. People who entertain notions of superhuman agency may well include these notions in their own description of why they do what they do during scripted, ritualized ceremonies, or what "meaning" it conveys. These are optional additions that do not explain any of the features of ritualized behavior or its effects in participants.

To return to our general theme, there seems to be a widespread belief that there is such a thing as "religious experience". But a careful consideration of the evidence leads to a deflated version of this view. Naturally, people who entertain thoughts about superhuman agents or perform behavior related to those imagined agents have experiences – the question is whether those are specific to such contexts. The study of exceptional experiences, such as altered

29 See BELL, *Ritual Theory, Ritual Practice* [1992].

states of consciousness, visions, etc., does not really warrant that assumption. Such states, to the extent that they are associated with discernible conceptual content, do not require religious thoughts. Non-exceptional experiences, such as participation in ritualized behavior, do not require religious concepts either. In both cases, it seems that religious thoughts are essentially parasitic on forms of behavior that can be explained without them.

5. Are religions against reason and freedom?

That religion is not, to put things mildly, the most efficient or successful way to understand the world, is not really contentious anymore. As I said at the beginning, we need not try to reinvent what the *Aufklärung* scholars did so well. But some Enlightenment questions remain and become ever more pressing in present circumstances, namely: Do religions have a positive impact on society? Are religious thought and behavior "bad" for human thought? for culture? for human societies? In what circumstances do beliefs in supernatural agents become harmless? Should one try to get rid of them? Is that possible?

A recapitulation of natural religious elements

It may be of help at this point to recapitulate the key conclusions of the scientific study of religious thought and behavior. Though the research program is still in its prime, it already provides us with a broad sketch with these essential points:

The way we acquire, store, organize religious concepts is to a large extent inaccessible to conscious inspection. This is not so surprising, since most cognitive processes are beyond conscious access. We do not know or experience how our visual cortices translate retinal images into the illusions of 3-D scenes. We do not know or experience how other cortical networks produce syntactic sentences. In the same way, we do not know or experience the processes whereby we attribute agency to unobserved agents, or moral judgments to those same imagined agents. The way to find out how this takes place is not, or not just, to ask people what their "beliefs" are – for people do not believe what they believe they believe. The only way is to run experiments, test models of cognitive structure, measure how well these models account for observed religious behavior.

Most religious concepts are parasitic upon mental systems that would be there, religion or not. Cognitive studies reach a similar conclusion in several distinct domains of religious thought. It turns out that having religious concepts does not require specific mechanisms in the mind in comparison with vision, or language comprehension, or the understanding of other people's emotions, all of which require specific functional structures. Religious cognition seems to be parasitic in the sense that all the systems involved in its acquisition and its mental effects would be there, religions or not.

Religious agency (gods, spirits, ancestors, etc.) belongs to a larger repertoire of "supernatural agents" defined as violations of intuitions about agents. The material composition of religions does not in this respect differ from that of folklore. There is a small repertoire of possible types of supernatural characters, most of whom are found in folktales and other minor cultural domains, though some of them belong to the important gods or spirits or ancestors of "religion". Most of these characters are explicitly defined by having counter-intuitive properties that violate general expectations about agents. They are sometimes undetectable, or prescient, or eternal. The way people represent such agents activates the enormous but inaccessible machinery of "theory of mind" and other mental systems that provide us with a representation of agents, their intentions and their beliefs. All this is inaccessible to conscious inspection and requires no social transmission. On the other hand, what is socially transmitted are the counter-intuitive features: this one is omniscient, that one can go through walls, another one was born of a virgin, etc.

Religious morality is parasitic upon non-religious moral intuitions. Developmental research shows the early appearance and systematic organization of moral intuitions: a set of precise feelings evoked by the consideration of actual and possible courses of action. Although people often state that their moral rules are a consequence of the existence of the decrees of supernatural agents, it is quite clear that such intuitions are present, independently of religious concepts. Moral intuitions appear long before children represent the powers of supernatural agents; they appear in the same way in cultures in which no-one is really interested in supernatural agents, and in similar ways regardless of what kind of supernatural agents are locally important. Indeed, it is difficult to find evidence that religious teachings have any effect on people's moral intuitions.

So far, we have considered the most important domains of religious thought and behavior – supernatural agency, ritual action, morality, misfortune – without mentioning what to some people is the *sine qua non* of religion. We have made no mention of transcendence, of infinite power, of cosmology, of how souls get saved or why evil exists. This is because such questions are blithely ignored by most people in most places in the world, and have been so for most of human history, as far as we can tell from the evidence. Religions do not exist because of the need to answer such questions, far from it. Such questions are a special, local development that arose in societies with guilds of religious specialists.

Is religion an adaptation? An evolutionary perspective implies that manifest behaviors are enabled and supported by functional systems which are the outcome of natural selection. In other words, some of these functional systems can be construed as adaptations, that is, reliably developing capacities or traits that provide evidence of complex functional design and confer potential reproductive advantages (or did so under ancestral conditions).[1] Also, the trait would have evolved gradually from previous versions, with adaptive advantages being conferred by each incremental change, as evolution does not look ahead. These stringent criteria mean that few functional features can be described as evolutionary adaptations. Note that general statements about adaptations and their by-products are conclusions, not starting points. Before we can say anything about the adaptive function of religious thoughts or behaviors, we have to analyze what makes them possible, which is the substantial contribution of the evidence reviewed in the preceding chapters.

Cognitive accounts of religion even suggest that there is no good reason for the existence of religious thoughts and behaviors. There is not even a unique cause for them. Rather, the most plausible scenario takes them as a by-product of a whole variety of cognitive adaptations, of mental systems that we have for good reason. This causal account clashes with most people's expectations, particularly with those of religious adherents. We generally tend to think that people perform a particular ritual for a reason: indeed, the first thing we researchers do is ask them what the reason is. But cognitive models seem to suggest that this is not the most profitable strategy, since the explanation for religious notions lies in processes that people cannot be aware of, so that the explicit reasons ("we sacrifice to the ancestors because they protect us") is at best a rationalization of thoughts and behaviors that would occur in the absence of such "reasons".

A believer may well think she has such concepts because they explain a lot, or because they are awesome and beautiful stories, or because life would make no sense if they were false, or because it makes her happy, or because most other people seem to accept them. All these are real consequences of having the concepts, but non-starters as explanations for why one acquired them in the first place and why they appeared in human cultures at all. This applies, obviously, just as well to the notion that people spontaneously and intuitively adhere to religious concepts because religious concepts are true. (One comes across this argument surprisingly often in debates about religion). Besides solving the delicate problem of deciding which religious concepts are true, between all the incompatible, mutually refuting versions available, proponents of this simple explanation also have to ignore two major facts of human history: there is no limit to the range of false concepts people can sincerely and intuitively find plausible; conversely, there is a vast domain of true concepts that our minds find it exceedingly difficult to acquire, as science shows every day. Given the colossal evidence for both tendencies, the fact that most humans find a particular representation is certainly no guarantee of validity, far from it.

---

1 Buss et al., *Adaptions, exaptations, and spandrels* [1998], 545; see WILLIAMS, *Adaption and Natural Selection* [1966].

Understanding religious cognition without "belief"

Most debates about the value and explanation of religion are couched in terms of belief and take it for granted that we know what we are talking about when we use that term. This, unfortunately, is far from being the case. There is no clear model in psychology of what belief is, or rather there are many different understandings specific to a variety of mental phenomena we usually lump under the common term of belief. In another book, I tried to describe and explain the "decentralized" model of belief that cognitive science puts forward.[2] This is an exceedingly difficult point to convey. The problem is that we have a commonsense notion of belief that is so entrenched in our ordinary ways of thinking about the mind that it is almost impossible for us not to use it, and to do so even when we are aware of how unsatisfactory it is.

Briefly, then: we typically consider beliefs to be statements that the person considers, judges to be true, and is disposed to act upon. This assumes that there is a kind of mental stage upon which these different statements or positions are exhibited, and there is a kind of audience – the person herself – to make the judgment. The problem is that all that is clearly false. In terms of cognitive processes, all there is are all kinds of information pieces, represented by activation patterns inside brains. These pieces of information are not considered by the mind, they are the mind. So it makes little sense to talk about the mind or the self or the person judging a proposition.[3] "Belief" (construed for instance as the disposition to assent to a particular statement, or to act on the basis of some information) is an emergent consequence of a myriad of computational processes that do not engage the conscious subject.

Let us then focus on those processes that may be relevant to understanding the emergence of thoughts about superhuman agents. Most religious statements are represented not as simple propositions ("p") but as complex formulae of the form "Proposition p is x", in which the "x" may stand for "true", "guaranteed by the ancestors", "said by the prophets", etc. In other words, such statements are meta-represented. They constitute "reflective beliefs", distinct from intuitive beliefs (e. g. that a table is a solid object) by the fact that reflective beliefs are explicitly represented along with comments on their validity.[4] This would suggest that two processes are involved in generating commitment to religious statements. First, particular statements are meta-represented, so that the propositional content is specifically linked to particular authorities, which may strengthen their plausibility even when the content is not entirely elucidated. Second, people establish particular

---

2 See Boyer, *Religion Explained* [2001].

3 See Stich, *From Folk-Psychology to cognitive Science* [1983].

4 Cosmides/Tooby, *Consider the source: The evolution of adaptions for decoupling and metarepresentation* [2000], 105 f; Sperber, *Intuitive and reflective beliefs* [1997], 82 f.

associations between these socially transmitted statements, particular events, and background cognitive principles – the kind of process I described in chapter 2. To sum up, discussions of religious thought and behavior gain very little by framing the issue in terms of "belief", and we would make great progress by abandoning the term and focusing on the actual cognitive processes at stake, those that make particular representations plausible and particular behaviors compelling.

Religion is not the sleep of reason

There is a long and respectable tradition of explaining religion as the consequence of a flaw in mental functioning. Because people do not think much or not very well, the argument goes, unwarranted beliefs are like unnecessary furniture in their minds. In other words, there is religion because people fail to take prophylactic measures against erroneous beliefs, for one of the following reasons:

People are superstitious, they will believe anything. Religious concepts are both cheap and sensational; they are easy to understand and rather exciting to entertain.

Religious concepts are irrefutable. As there is no evidence against most religious claims, people have no obvious reason to stop believing them.

Refutation is more difficult than belief. It takes greater effort to challenge and rethink established notions than just accept them. If everyone around you says that there are invisible dead people around, and everyone acts accordingly, it would take a much greater effort to try and verify such claims than it takes to accept them, if only provisionally.

I find all these arguments unsatisfactory. Not that they are false: religious claims are indeed beyond verification. People do like sensational supernatural tales better than banal stories and they generally spend little time rethinking every bit of cultural information they acquire. But this cannot be a sufficient explanation for why people have the concepts they have, the beliefs they have, the emotions they have. The idea that we are often gullible or superstitious is certainly true; but we are not gullible in just every possible way. People do not generally strive to believe six impossible things before breakfast, as does the White Queen in Lewis Carroll's *Through the Looking-Glass*. Religious claims are irrefutable, but so are all sorts of other far-fetched notions that we never find in religion. Religion is not a domain where anything goes, where any strange belief could appear and get transmitted from generation to generation. On the contrary, there is only a limited catalog of possible supernatural and religious beliefs.

Taking all this into account, it would seem that the "sleep of reason" interpretation of religion is less than compelling. It is quite clear that explicit religious belief requires a suspension of the sound rules according to which most scientists evaluate evidence. But so does most ordinary thinking of the kind that sustains our commonsense intuitions about the surrounding environment. More surprising, religious notions are not at all a separate realm of cognitive activity. They are firmly rooted in the deepest principles of cognitive functioning. First, religious concepts would not be salient if they did not violate some of our most entrenched intuitions (e. g., that agents have a position in space, that live beings grow old and die, etc.). Second, religious concepts would not subsist if they did not confirm many intuitive principles. Third, most religious norms and emotions are parasitic upon systems that create very similar norms (e. g., moral intuitions) and emotions (e. g., a fear of invisible contaminants) in non-religious contexts.

In this sense, religious thought is vastly more "natural" than the "sleep of reason" argument would suggest. The "tweaking" of ordinary cognition that is required to sustain religious thought is so minimal that one should not be surprised if religious concepts are so widespread and so resistant to argument. To some extent, the situation is similar to domains where science has clearly demonstrated the limits or falsity of our common intuitions. We now know that solid objects are largely made up of empty space, that our minds are only billions of neurons firing in ordered ways, that some physical processes can go backwards in time, that species do not have an eternal essence, that gravitation is a curvature of space-time. Yet even scientists go through their daily lives with an intuitive commitment to solid objects being full of matter, to people having non-physical minds, to time being irreversible, to cats being essentially different from dogs, and to objects falling down because they are heavy.

The troubled consciousness of modern religions

It is often said of members of a minority that they live in two different worlds, that of their own community and that of the world at large. These worlds differ in terms of language, values, ways of speaking and other norms. Black children in the United States, for instance, often speak two very different dialects of English, maintain two different conversational styles and cultural preferences, and gradually learn to negotiate smooth transitions from one "world" to the other. To a large degree, members of religious institutions in modern societies live in a comparable situation. In highly secularized places like Europe, but also to a large degree in the United States, religious people know that one should not talk or behave oneself in the same way, in and out of the community of the faithful. There are things one can say inside that would not pass muster outside. It is all right for instance for Europeans to say "I am a Christian", but it would seem terribly odd if people said, in a matter of fact way, that "God is listening to me" or "I asked God for advice". But they can make the latter statements once they are back inside the group. Many Christians will readily admit that the picture of an omniscient wise old man listening to their prayers is a bit childish, and will add that "of course that is not what religion is about", adding that both theology and the faith of ordinary believers are far from that childish stereotype. Yet, once they are back with fellow believers, they express all sorts of beliefs that are exactly of that format. This was noticed and commented on, with characteristic acuity, by Richard Dawkins after many others.[5] Dawkins sees that as some form of hypocrisy, a denial of the true – and truly childish – nature of most religious beliefs. We can perhaps explain it more economically as the need for members of religious institutions to adopt the dialect of a highly secularized culture.

This need to adapt to the outside may lead to strange conceptual contortions. Some time ago, the British magazine *Spectator* polled a number of bishops in the Church of England about Easter, asking them whether it was true that "Christ has risen from the dead". Almost all of the bishops replied with some formula along the lines of "It is a tenet of our Christian tradition that resurrection happened" – to which the journalist would retort, "yes, yes, I know that it is your tradition, but I am asking you about a fact: has it happened?" This would be greeted by something like "To me as Christian, it is an important tenet of my faith that the Scriptures convey an important truth when they tell us that Christ rose from the dead." A renewed request for a definite statement about what had happened would be met with the same kind of contorted rhetoric. Only very few of the bishops, after repeated badgering, would concede that, yes, as far as they were concerned, Christ had actually risen from the dead. The circumvolutions are actually founded on a simple premise. The religious officer is not saying that "such-and-such is the case", but that "it is true (beautiful, mysterious, symbolic, traditional, etc.) that 'such and such is the case'".

This proliferation of meta-statements is endemic to many Western religious institutions, particularly in Europe, and for good reason. Any one who makes a statement like "so and so has risen from the dead" and wants to present it as a historical fact, is just asking for cognitive grief. Extraordinary statements demand extraordinarily good evidence, and no-one takes "it is written in the Book" or "the institution says it did happen" as any kind of evidence any longer. Obviously, the same goes for many other religious statements that are officially part of the canon, but are generally discreetly papered over by most religious personnel, as slightly embarrassing or obviously false in their literal meaning, therefore to be treated as "symbolic" or "mysterious". As Karl Kraus pointed out,

---

5 See DAWKINS, *The God Delusion* [2006].

A lightning conductor on top of a church is the strongest possible vote of no-confidence against dear God [...][6]

which sums up the problem of maintaining both metaphysical beliefs and some commitment in the everyday validity of science in the same context. Kierkegaard, as we noted above, was fond of the notion of religious commitment as *cognitive offense*, as an unacceptable proposition that one needs to hold, in the same way as Abraham was coerced into the morally unacceptable decision of taking his son's life.[7] But this attitude seems to be absent from the religious life of most members of modern religious institutions. The *credo quia absurdum*, that is, I *have* to believe these propositions because reason revolts against them, is replaced with a "I believe as long as I can make the claims ambiguous enough".

This attitude of mental restriction is all the more striking as it conflicts with the contents of most institutionalized religion. For instance, it seems extremely difficult both to take seriously the tenets of Christianity and accept that one's Christian faith is a private matter. The faith in question, after all, contains very clear warnings about the risks of particular behaviors, and makes it a duty to inform others of what they should do. Indeed the whole message is framed in terms of a "good news" that *must* be conveyed to all those who unfortunately have not heard or understood it yet. So the religious person should, as a direct inference of what they believe, make a point of telling others about the message, especially those who do not profess any religious belief. One should not leave them alone, any more than one should "leave alone" a person drowning in a lake or about to fall from a cliff.

The consequence of such difficult tensions is a kind of double consciousness, in which people can both claim that particular statements about the world, salvation, etc, are absolute truths, while in practice they live as though these elements of doctrine were optional. This leads also to many of the contorted reasoning described above, in which one tries to escape from the tension by making religion "symbolic" or "inspiring" or "profound", that is, by making it essentially empty.

Two escape routes – fundamentalism and "spirituality"

Contrast the sorry plight of modern religious institutions in the West with the healthy (so to speak – at least, robust) certainty of other traditions. The phenomena I described above are precisely what fundamentalist movements despise most and try to undermine. In the worldview of a fundamentalist,

---

6 KRAUS: „Ein Blitzableiter auf einem Kirchturm ist das denkbar stärkste Mißtrauensvotum gegen den lieben Gott [...]" *Sprüche und Widersprüche* [1909], 43.
7 See KIERKEGAARD, *Either/Or: A Fragment of Life* [1992].

there are no pusillanimous retreats into the private world, or tortuous cognitive adjustments between metaphysical urgency and social acceptability.[8] Fundamentalists take the contents of institutional religious messages seriously, as saying what they say and prescribing what they prescribe. If one had belief in the text as a sacred scripture and the text says that a particular behavior *is* abominable, then it is abominable, whatever polite society says about it, and it *must* be eradicated – and in the meantime one must persuade others that the behavior indeed *is* abominable.

Compared to many forms of modern institutional religion, fundamentalism is of course strikingly (indeed stridently) coherent. It does not require the multiple equivocations that allow supernatural claims to pass muster in a modern environment. The whole point of most fundamentalist movements is to *reestablish* a direct commitment to the main propositions of a religious institution. Despite important cultural differences, fundamentalisms of the world do share important features, one of which is the desire to "return" to a largely mythical past, when people's beliefs were not troubled by modern notions of evidence and pragmatic efficacy. This is true of course of Islamic and Christian fundamentalists, but also of less salient movements like the Hindu reformist schools.

Fundamentalisms are by nature subversive and reactionary movements, but it is a misleading simplification to see them primarily as a revolt against "modernity". Modern life ways by themselves are not so much the target of such movements, which generally make good use of whatever modern technology can serve their purposes. Rather than modernity, the target is the weakened commitment typical of modern religious institutions.[9] That may be why most fundamentalist movements are, to a large degree, more interested in other members of their own religious traditions than in outsiders. The most important audience that Muslim or Christian fundamentalists want to reach is of course that of weakly committed Muslims or Christians.

Most religious reformers, fundamentalists included, try to impose a religious order, coerce people into submission, and generally use political means, legitimate or not, towards that goal.[10] This preoccupation with eliminating the non-fundamentalist, weakly committed religious alternative, makes sense in view of what we know of human commitment strategies (see chapter 3). A recurrent problem of coalitions is that people may defect, which of course would be costly for the other, more committed members of the coalition. A recurrent solution or palliative is to make defection potentially very costly. This makes intuitive sense to most people engaged in coalitional

---

8 See LAWRENCE, Defenders of God: *The Fundamentalist Revolt against the Modern Age* [1989]; MARTY/APPLEBY, *Fundamentalisms observed* [1991]; MARTY/APPLEBY, *Fundamentalism and Society* [1993]; MARTY/APPLEBY, *Fundamentalism and the State* [1993]; MARTY/APPLEBY, *Accounting for Fundamentalisms* [1994].
9 See BOYER, *Religion Explained* [2001].
10 See MARTY/APPLEBY, *Fundamentalism and Society* [1993].

affiliation, even though they do not have explicit, consciously accessible representations of the game-theoretic aspects of strategic commitment. Consider how politically engaged people routinely despise and distrust people who leave their parties because of disagreement with the official "line" or decisions, and conversely admire those who stick with the party despite similar divergence. The same is true of religious coalitions – apostates, like renegades, are just not acceptable. Note that this would make no sense from the standpoint of religious doctrine – why should people who do not adhere to the institutions' proclaimed beliefs stay in the fold? But these attitudes are perfectly tuned to coalitional strategies. The loathing, and even better the public humiliation or deprecation of defectors increases the cost of defection and therefore reduces its likelihood.

Coalitional psychology also explains the doctrinal stridency of fundamentalists. Given that they construe membership in their groups as a high-cost, subversive, minority endeavor, it makes sense for them to insist on precisely those aspects of the doctrine that are most ridiculous or repulsive for outsiders. These serve the function of commitment signals. By accepting such extreme versions of the religious system, indeed proclaiming them, recruits signal that they are ready to pay the necessary cost to be members of the group. This would not work as a commitment signal if the doctrine in question was a mild, nuanced version that anyone could be comfortable with. The doctrine therefore must be cognitively shocking – and therefore highly literal, when the scriptures of the group include many obviously absurd statements.

The untenable situation of modern religions – the fact that some of their central claims are just too odd to be taken seriously even by participants in the institutions – also results in the opposite reaction, in a retreat into comfortable vagueness. To many people, it seems too narrow or uninspiring to talk about "religious" doctrines, experience and feelings. This seems to be a plausible explanation for the increased popularity of the notion of "spirituality", and a "spiritual life". The origins of this usage are intriguing (they link to the spread of "spiritualism" in Europe and America at the turn of the twentieth-century). But the present usage is even more interesting. In many contexts, people have come to talk about spirituality and spiritual experience where they used to speak of religion and religious experience. Why is that the case?

The obvious starting point would be to try and understand what people mean when they talk about spirituality – and there the problems begin. Consider the following statements:

Spirituality [...] touches the core of our human existence: our relation to the Absolute.[11]

---

11 WAAIJMAN, *Spirituality: Forms, Foundations, Methods* [2002], 10.

Spirituality is a way of life that affects and includes every moment of existence. It is at once a contemplative attitude, a disposition to a life of depth, and the search for ultimate meaning, direction, and belonging.[12]

Spirituality is the inherent aspect of our human *beingness*. [...] Spirituality impels us to seek and to discover the *more* of who we are and calls us to enter the depths of our own being, where we discover our intrinsic connectedness with all of life and with the eternal Oneness and Sacred Source of our being.[13]

Obviously, conceptual precision is not among the top priorities in this domain. What exactly is "connectedness" or the "sacred source of our being"? A major difference between theology and spirituality-talk, it would seem, is that the latter has abandoned even the intention to talk about anything in particular. The above excerpts, in their frustrating lack of discernible meaning, are sadly typical of the free-wheeling metaphorical expanse characteristic of that field. Frequently repeated terms like "oneness" or "ultimate" periodically signal to readers that some kind of metaphysics is the overall topic, without conveying any of the contents of that metaphysics. That is what linguists would call a purely "indexical" use of metaphysical concepts.

The vagueness here is not just a problem of expression. Far from being the accidental outcome of some authors' particularly poor writing, there is in general a deep reluctance in this field to commit oneself to any specific claim. I strongly suspect – this is largely speculative – that that is precisely what drives the whole field of "spirituality". The whole point of spirituality-talk, it seems, is to *avoid* particular topics rather than address them. And I further suspect that those topics are, as it happens, what constitutes standard religious thoughts and behaviors. Let me provide more excerpts:

Religion and spirituality are not mutually exclusive, but there is a real difference. [...] Spirituality [...] requires some sort of spiritual practice that acts as a catalyst to inner change and growth.[14]

You can walk a wonderful spiritual path with or without adhering to a religion. All paths are equally available. None are exclusively right or wrong or even required.[15]

The real religion of mankind can be said to be spirituality itself. [Spirituality] acknowledges the place of ultimate reality in all the religions of the world. It expresses this truth in the following words: "The world religions bear witness to the experience of Ultimate Reality to which they give various names, Brahman, Allah, the Absolute, God, Great Spirit".[16]

---

12 TEASDALE, *The Mystic Heart: Discovering a Universal Spirituality in the World's Religions* [1999], 11.
13 BURKHARDT/NAGAI-JACOBSON, *Spirituality: Living our Connectedness* [2001], 4.
14 TEASDALE, *The Mystic Heart* [1999], 10.
15 LESSER, *The New American Spirituality* [1999], xv.
16 TEASDALE, *The Mystic Heart* [1999], 14.

Despite the confused metaphors, one can extract two fundamental ideas from the spirituality literature. One is that the life of the spirit, whatever that is, is something *broader* or *deeper* than the usual content of religions. The spatial metaphor is recurrent in this literature. The second is that, from that "deeper" perspective, all religions can be seen as equivalent. This suggests that religions with their particular claims and rituals should be, if not abandoned, at least demoted as a source of important information and experience.

Clearly, such claims constitute a frontal attack on religions, the products and services delivered and guaranteed by religious guilds. These institutions, as I explained in the first chapter, are founded on the notion of a specific, and necessarily exclusive type of ritual or conceptual service. From the point of view of participants in such institutions, it makes little sense to say that "no [religions] are exclusively right or wrong", as participation is based on recognition of a highly specific version of religious thoughts and behaviors as the only appropriate one. Also, the point of having religious guilds is that they provide all of the religious services – which is why they are so often involved in suppressing alternative cults, syncretism and local mediums. So the notion of religious development as a personal affair is of course a clear threat to religious guilds, like home improvement is to carpenters or private militias to the state.

In most economically advanced societies, there is a tacit understanding that most religious claims belong to the same category as fairy tales. That is because most religious pronouncements about actual things in the world, about how the world works (as opposed to statements about invisible processes), turned out to be wrong. That has been an embarrassment for religious institutions for some time, and has created all sorts of special attitudes that I described above: the notion that religious claims are "symbolic", that they should be "inspiring" rather than descriptive, and so on. It seems that "spirituality" is another example of that attitude. Some people seem to like all the ways of thinking and the ways of feeling, that religion used to bring with it such as: the focus on extremely big questions – and on extraordinarily simple and vague answers; a specific kind of emotion in which we participate in other people's thoughts; an impression that we go beyond the domains of practical and everyday thoughts; finally, an aesthetic of sonorous empathy. All these used to be provided by institutional religion. But, as most religious institutions got caught making patently false claims about the world, and because they foster metaphysical claims that people these days find, rather far-fetched, there is a demand for some way of having all of the benefits listed above without associating them with the slightly ridiculous aspects of institutional religion. The word "spirituality", which seems to convey some of the positive (or rather, supposedly positive) aspects of religion without any of what most people would see as "mumbo-jumbo".

No need for "science and religion" or different "magisteria"

Should there be a "dialog" between science and religions? In the light of all the empirical evidence presented here, it would seem that this very notion of a "debate" or "confrontation" or even comparison is hopelessly confused. I will leave aside the strange assumptions about science that are usually made in this context, and focus on the other side of the supposed debate. As I said above, most debates of this kind naturally assume that there is such a thing as religion – and maintain a constant ambiguity between religious thoughts and behaviors, phenomena that we find in many cultures and many people, on the one hand, and religious institutions, the guilds of specialists found in some contexts, with their official doctrines and prescriptions. Moreover, a comparison or contrast only makes sense against some background of similarity, but there is none between scientific theories, held and understood by a very small number of people in a small number of human groups, and the religious imagination, easily acquired and maintained by millions of people with no effort. A more sensible comparison would be between scientific activity and theology, or between popular representations of science and popular religiosity on the other.[17]

The latter comparison makes great sense – as an anthropological problem of cultural transmission. Scientific research and theorizing has appeared only in very few human societies. Wherever it is done, it requires massive effort and institutional support, and it does not seem accessible to more than a small minority of people. The results of scientific research may be well-known, but the whole intellectual style that is required to achieve them is really difficult to acquire.[18] By contrast, religious representations have appeared in all human groups that we know, they are easily acquired, they are maintained effortlessly and they seem accessible to all members of a group, regardless of intelligence or training. As Robert McCauley points out, this and many other features of the two domains suggest that religious representations are highly natural to human beings, while science is quite clearly unnatural.[19] That is, the former goes with the grain of our evolved intuitions, while the latter requires that we suspend, or even contradict most of our common ways of thinking. So it makes sense to see these two domains as diametrical examples of cultural transmission, two limiting-cases in the connections between evolved cognition and cultural creations.

However, that is not in general what people want from a "science and religion debate". The point of such debates is usually a comparison between theological doctrines and scientific theories. Obviously, we are not in pre-

---

17 McCAULEY, *The naturalness of religion and the unnaturalness of science* [2000], 71 f.
18 WOLPERT, *The Unnatural Nature of Science* [1992], XI-XII.
19 McCAULEY, *The naturalness of religion and the unnaturalness of science* [2000], 64.

Enlightenment times any longer, so no-one expects religious institutions to provide reliable information about the way the world works. There is no "debate" in the sense that scientific developments have made all religiously inspired pronouncements about the world simply unnecessary. What could be gained then by comparing them to scientific discoveries? A common response is that the whole point of the debate is to clarify the proper domains of these two kinds of intellectual activity. An example of this type of argument is Stephen J. Gould's description of science and religion as two "non-overlapping magisteria"[20], not so much an original concept as the clearest formulation of a very common opinion, viz. that science should teach us about the domain of empirical fact, while religions are concerned with meaning and value, metaphysics and morality. In Gould's essay, this demarcation is intended both as a description and as a norm, as what these two kinds of human activity actually do and what they should stick to.

However seeming innocuous this division of labor between scientific research and religious doctrines, it is rather misguided in both descriptive or normative terms. It seems confused for two reasons: first, it is not at all clear that issues of values and morality necessarily fall outside the domain of science; second, even when they do, it is not clear at all that religious doctrines are a relevant source to resolve them.

Consider the thorny issue of abortion. In some countries (especially in the U.S., and especially for religious folks), there is still an intense debate about abortion, generally phrased in terms of respect for "human life", as opposed to respect for women's lives and choices. To some people, it seems clearly abhorrent that one could decide to eliminate a fetus – and others do not share that intuition, however regrettable they find abortions. One of the implicit, perhaps inaccessible reasons for this divergence is a difference in intuitions about persons. Indeed, the rhetoric of anti-abortion movements is generally peppered with reference to personhood ("killing a baby"), while the other side is more comfortable with biological facts (e. g. that normal function of a woman's body does result in numerous undetected abortions).

Now consider the science. One thing we know, from experimental studies in moral psychology, is that people's emotions and judgments are only loosely related to general principles, so that the "sacredness of life" is probably not the deductive origin of people's rejection of all abortions in principle. In general, moral principles serve as justification, or *ex post facto* rationalization of prior intuitions and emotions.[21] Also, clever experiments show that people do not generally hold that particular principle (that all human life is sacred) as absolute. When confronted with vignettes in which one has to choose between

20 See GOULD, *Nonoverlapping Magisteria: science and religion are not in conflict, for their teachings occupy distinctly different domains* [1997].
21 GREENE, *Cognitive neuroscience and the structure of the moral mind* [2005], 348 f; HAIDT, *The new synthesis in moral psychology* [2007], 1000.

sacrificing a life and, e.g. allowing others to survive, most defenders of the sacredness of life end up making choices that are sensitive to the context.[22]

So what seems to make the debates intractable is different intuitions about what makes an aggregate of biological tissue a *person*. If the embryo is a person, it seems horrendous to condone its termination for the sake of another person's welfare – although of course there may be extreme circumstances where that might be considered. If the embryo is only the *possibility* or the *starting point* of a person, then the act though deplorable is not intrinsically criminal. But this is where science is helpful too. When debates about abortion mention scientific findings – to the extent that that happens, which is very rare – these come from medicine and physiology. But that is not quite relevant to the issue of deciding personhood. More pertinent results come from experimental and developmental psychology, showing how we spontaneously attribute *personhood* but also other features, like *animacy, awareness* and *moral value* to particular organisms in our environment. Why do we think that there is sentience in other adult human beings, and some form of it in infants and non-human animals? How do we judge that cats and dogs behave the way they do because they want to, whereas amoebas and sponges do not?

In brief, the evidence suggests that (1) the notion of a person is made up of different features, (2) each of these is the result of complex inferences; there is no straightforward criterion in any case, and (3) the way these intuitions are put together varies from place to place and in function of people's circumstances. Also, this research shows that the person concept is emphatically normative. It describes the way a certain class of agents is supposed to function, such that, among other things, we can attribute moral value to their actions.[23] That is why there is and can be no straightforward demarcation between persons and non-persons.[24]

So at least some scientific facts are relevant to what would seem to belong to the moral "magisterium". Sure, the science, in this case, in the form of psychological findings, seems mostly to tell us why the debate is intractable, rather than provide an easy solution. However, it would seem urgent to include such scientific evidence in the debates, if only to stop people from assuming that there is a fact of the matter where there isn't one. Science, in essence, tells us that the relevant decisions about personhood, in tragic circumstances like abortion but also in cases of euthanasia, are most likely the outcome of a complex negotiation between mental systems, none of which provides a clear solution.

---

22 Foot, *Killing, letting die, and euthanasia* [1981]; Thomson, *A defense of abortion* [1971].

23 See Matthews, *Personal identity, multiple personality disorder, and moral personhood* [1998]; Scott, *Moral Personhood: An Essay in the Philosophy of Moral Psychology* [1990].

24 See Doris/Knobe/Woolfolk, *Variantism about responsibility* [2007]; Jack/Robbins, *The illusory triumph of machine over mind* [2004].

That is why, also, it would probably be foolish to hope that religions can step in and provide guidance in such matters. How could doctrines associated with supernatural agency any longer provide, criteria for personhood? Gould's notion of a moral "magisterium" suggests that religions (as well as philosophical doctrines) constitute a source of moral understandings. But, as I tried to show in a previous chapter, that is far from obvious. Religious doctrines provide codified morality and moral exemplars, people of great virtue whom one is supposed to emulate. But neither of these seems terribly important to people's actual decision-making. By contrast, what people take from religious thought is the notion of superhuman agents that have a stake in our decisions. That is the main way in which they associate superhuman agents to moral decisions. Beliefs such as "The ancestors are watching", or "the gods may be guiding us" provide a context in which moral decisions are made in front of an imagined audience, so to speak. Now, as I said before, none of our intuitive moral understandings actually require any concept of superhuman agency – indeed, they are found in similar form in believers and non-believers, in children and in adults the world over. Morality does not need religious thoughts – but religious thoughts are often parasitic on evolved moral intuitions.

That is probably why the contribution of established religions to such debates as the legal status of abortion is, in terms of content, rather poor. In Islam for instance, the issue is determined on the basis of a pre-biological theory of "ensoulment". Various schools, however, differ on the circumstances under which an embryo can be sacrificed.[25] Classical Hinduism would be tolerant of early abortions under the principle of doing the least harm, weighing the woman's health against that of the embryo.[26] Theological disquisitions of this kind (Christian specialists say more or less the same thing) are of little value in decision-making, and in the end leave each group or person with the intuitions about personhood that they would have anyway, religion or not.

I insisted on the notion of "non-overlapping magisteria" because it points to the kind of intellectual limitation that is unfortunately typical of many discussions of "science and religion". That is, the whole discussion here starts from the assumption that institutional religious doctrine on the one hand, and scientific inquiry on the other, are the only ways in which we organize knowledge of the world. Another assumption is that if a particular question is not handled by one of these "magisteria" then it surely belongs to the other. Neither assumption is warranted.

---

25 See Musallam, *Sex and Society in Islam* [1983].
26 See Coward/Lipner/Young, *Hindu Ethics: Purity, Abortion, and Euthanasia* [1989].

Two varieties of Enlightenment

Ernest Gellner once argued that there are at least two versions of the Enlightenment, what he called the *vulgar* and *sophisticated* versions respectively.[27] The vulgar vision was put forward, as Gellner points out, by people who were far from being vulgar themselves – the French *philosophes* and other intellectuals who advocated a resolutely materialistic and rationalist worldview, and pursued religion with the most relentless sarcasm. These early debunkers, Voltaire foremost among them, had no time for what later generations would call the "mumbo-jumbo" of institutional religion, i. e. the bizarre or simply absurd beliefs that seem to crop up in most religious systems. There is certainly no more powerful argument against the Christian dogma than Voltaire's scrupulous enumeration of all the strange things a believer is enjoined to accept. His descriptions of theological disputes would be unsurpassable (except that reality in this domain often surpasses the best efforts of satirists).[28] The French *philosophes* had great weapons – the unconstrained use of reason, the beginnings of the scientific revolution, as well as much new scholarship in the history of religion – to attack established religion, and they used them with great gusto and unsurpassed efficacy. However, the *philosophes* did not have much of an explanation for religious belief. They were very good at pointing out where reason supposedly fails, but not why it does so, and even less why it does so in such recurrent fashion. They were great polemicists and poor psychologists – even the greatest, like d'Alembert, could not find any other explanation for supernatural belief than the confusion of ill-trained minds.

That was precisely the great strength of the "sophisticated" Enlightenment, to use Gellner's term, especially of Hume and Smith and the general Scottish-English movement. Kant too can be counted among these 'sophisticated Enlightenment' figures, given his meticulous examination of the powers and limitations of human reason. These philosophers of course agreed with Voltaire or Diderot that religious traditions could not claim to be a sound way of understanding the world – that much was obvious from the development, however faltering at the time, of the natural sciences. They also started from a healthy skepticism directed at the excesses of religious doctrines – see Hume's essay on miracles.[29] But the question, then, was to understand how belief could be compelling, which required no less than a systematic account of how minds construct beliefs about the external world – which is what these early psychologists proceeded to explore.

27 See GELLNER, *Relativism and the Social Sciences* [1985].
28 See VOLTAIRE, *Dictionnaire philosphique* [1764].
29 See HUME, *Dialogues Concerning Natural Religion* [1779].

Now what do we need? We learned a great deal from David Hume and Adam Smith. Indeed, as I said several times, we are in debt to Kant and the Scottish Enlightenment, in terms of how societies work, how minds come to entertain ideas and believe them, including why religious thoughts ever occur to human beings and why they find them compelling. This enormous intellectual achievement is overwhelming, in comparison to the rather meager fare offered by the French *philosophes*, who just not in the same league as far as moral or political philosophy or epistemology are concerned. Yet the latter's political impact was enormous. More than the substance of what they said, Voltaire and materialists like Diderot changed civilized discourse forever by showing that individual intelligence did not have to submit to received traditions, or that doctrines that insult one's intelligence deserve only the scorn they receive. In other words, the *philosophes* did a great service to civil society by simply demonstrating that a certain kind of discourse was conceivable.

Popular modern atheists belong to this tradition of "vulgar Enlightenment" (again, no offense intended – there are worse things than being lumped together with Voltaire and Diderot).[30] They make the case that most pronouncements of religious traditions are, on the face of it, clearly false or downright ridiculous. Their opponents generally say that (1) the case they make is far from subtle, (2) it has been made many times before, so they are not even original, and (3) it is unlikely to persuade anyone who was not convinced already. These authors, like their eighteenth-century predecessors, are clearly not trying to understand how religions work or what made them culturally successful. Indeed their explanations often reduce to the idea that people are unintelligent or unimaginative. As we saw above, these are not very good explanations, to say the least.

All these objections to modern militant atheists are valid but also completely irrelevant. The point of militancy or advocacy is not to be subtle, original or profound; it is to bring about particular results. Now the result, though perhaps not the motivation, of atheist militants is an important one. In the same way as Voltaire was inaugurating a particular position for public intellectuals, modern atheists are trying to maintain the visibility of a particular intellectual position (that religion is intrinsically ridiculous) and by implication of a certain kind of discussion (e. g. of moral issues without the help of superhuman agency) and a certain kind of existence (a life without constraints from religious institutions). That, I think, is a positive outcome by itself, and I would claim, it is so even for religious believers, once we consider the modern relations between religious institutions and civil society.

---

30 See DAWKINS, *The God Delusion* [2006]; HITCHENS, *God is Not Great* [2007].

Misleading policies: the specificity of "religion"

Many issues in politics are construed in terms of relations between civil society, or the state, or the education, or judicial systems, on the one hand, and "religion" on the other. That is not the most promising beginning. Indeed, to the extent that public policy debate should be grounded in the best knowledge of the facts available, it is rather a disaster. Most social scientists would agree that "religion" is not a very useful category, especially as it combines and confuses corporate institutions (the religious groups and "guilds"), social groups (the membership of different religious affiliations), and a whole, vaguely defined set of thoughts and behaviors that are certainly not confined to those institutions and groups. A sure way to generate confused policy debates is to have them focused on quasi-mythical objects, which unfortunately is often the case, and particularly here.

In particular, talk of "religion" is misleading because it takes for granted two assumptions that are less than plausible – but belong to the religious institutions' doctrines. One is that religion is a unified package of morality, metaphysics and group identity – that is less than altogether compelling, as I argued in the first chapter. The other one is that religion is *sui generis*, that activities and institutions that belong to that vaguely defined category are of a special kind, not amenable to the categories and principles applied to other human activities.

To take a simple example, "religions" in the United States and some other countries are granted tax exemptions which, in strict terms, are the equivalent of public subsidies. As befits a place of great religious diversity and competition, all sorts of groups and institutions in the U.S. benefit from that indirect subsidy, from staid Protestant denominations to the outer fringe of crystal-gazers, from the most reassuring to the most sinister; to many outsiders it comes a surprise that the Scientology cult is an established "religion" in America. Now one might think, especially in such a bureaucratic and regulation-obsessed place as the U.S., that this provision is the result of a careful definition or legal understanding of what a religion is. Far from that being the case, it has been a constant of American history that this complicated issue is in practice handled by the tax authorities, since tax-exemption is the context in which the problem occurs. In practice, then, a group of civil servants with no required expertise beyond knowledge of the tax code routinely establishes that particular institutions and groups qualify as "religions", on the basis of the most intuitive criteria. They cannot expect much help from the apex of the American judicial system, as the United States Supreme Court has consistently avoided giving a clear definition of religion. In cases involving religious freedom (protected by the First and Fourteenth amendments), the court has for instance claimed that a characteristic of religion was the *sincerity* with which people hold their beliefs. So a group people who claimed to have supernatural healing powers, and charged for performance of their services, could benefit from state protection if they were sincere in their delusion. Otherwise they would be simple charlatans.[31] More recently, court opinions have maintained that *only* religious beliefs have certain privileges and protections, but still without providing any helpful hint as to what makes a particular belief religious.[32] Indeed, an important suggestion from the Court was that one should find inspiration from known exemplars. If a system of ideas has the same role for a person as traditionally recognized examples of religions have for their members, then that system probably *is* a religion.[33] The criterion amounts to what philosophers would call a "family resemblance" and taxonomists a "polythetic classification".[34] There is no hard and fast definition of a religion, but anything that looks or sounds like what you would usually call a religion must be one.

These semi-comical legal convolutions point to the problems one finds oneself into when attempting to define what is an object of postulation rather than observation or inference. As I argued at length, there simply is no such thing as "religion" in any sense that could serve as the basis for policy or indeed political theory. There is something worrying, and in fact downright dangerous, in policies or legal rules that stray beyond observable phenomena. To take a simple and innocuous example, it would seem that it is probably no business of the legal system or government to decide what is and what is not music. However, in some European countries in the 1980 s the popularity of "raves", large improvised parties where loud music and recreational drugs were the main attraction, prompted legislators to try and outlaw or at least contain that particular social phenomenon. This posed a difficult problem in that one cannot simply ban any gathering of like-minded people having fun, or allow the police to disband any such gathering whenever they feel like it. So one needed some criterion of what a rave was, and therefore some definition of music, the essential ingredient and the *raison d'etre* of these parties. The Westminster parliament duly passed the *U.K. Criminal Justice and Public Order Act* which specifies that special restrictions apply

to gathering on land, in the open air, of 100 or more persons at which amplified music is played during the night. Music includes sounds wholly or predominantly characterised by the emission of a succession of repetitive beats.[35]

---

31 SUPREME COURT, *United States v. Ballard, U.S. 78* [1944], 322.
32 SUPREME COURT, *Thomas v. Review Board, U.S. 707* [1981], 450.
33 SUPREME COURT, *Thomas v. Seeger, U.S. 63* [1965], 380.
34 See NEEDHAM, *Polythetic classification: convergence and consequences* [1975].
35 HOUSE OF COMMONS, *Art. 63(1)* [1994].

Much ridicule greeted this parliamentary definition of music, which is remarkable in being both false and partly circular (the notion of "beat" is intrinsically musical). The point, however, is that the law is bound to be asinine when it meddles in socially defined matters. There may well be objective features that define musical production, but they are only vaguely related to what people choose to call "music" at any one time. And that is why the law has no business dealing with the latter phenomenon.

The same point applies to "religion". The term does not denote any specific kind of material object, property, behavior, contract, corporation – in brief, it designates none of the kinds of things laws apply to. Having laws protecting or granting exceptions to "religion" is therefore bound to create either redundant regulations or unfair ones. The laws are in principle redundant when they, for instance, guarantee the freedom of religious expression when freedom of expression is guaranteed anyway, or the freedom of religious organization in countries where there is freedom of association to start with. (Obviously, there were good historical reasons for creating such special laws; but my point is about the present situation). When the laws about religion are not redundant, they are blatantly unfair. The U.S. legal system grants a tax exemption to any group that celebrates superhuman agents but none to groups that deny their existence. Scientology is therefore subsidized but not the *Scientific Committee for the Examination of Claims to the Paranormal*, for the reason that the latter only fosters verifiable beliefs. This unfairness is compounded by "anti-blasphemy" laws, as these protect murderous fanatics but not those who try to oppose them. Finally, the existence of a legal status for "religion" means that the state is actively helping established religious institutions, corporate groups with doctrines, buildings, corporate identities, etc., in their fight against the competition in the shape of self-styled mediums, independent gurus, free-lance shamans and such like (see chapter 1). There is no clear reason why the state should favor one type of religious thought and behavior against others – but that seems the inevitable result of trying to give "religion" a legal status that it does not need.

Political psychology and secularization

In these lectures I have not considered all aspects of the modern development of religious institutions, but only those we can understand better by paying attention to scientific evidence for our evolved mental capacities. Among those, I think we can include some reflections on the possible place of religious thoughts and behaviors, but also of religious institutions, in modern institutions, particularly as concerns the relations between state and civil society.

It has been only a few decades since political science converted to a systematic study of agents' interactions, mostly based on game-theory and other formal tools.[36] More recently, political scientists have gone further than a strictly normative formal approach, by considering the psychological processes underlying political attitudes and decisions.[37] So these are recent developments – the scientific part of political science is still in its infancy. Yet it may allow us to make minimal claims about the psychological processes involved in political decisions, in particular about the relationships between civil society and religions.

The question is classically construed in terms of "secularization", the modern move towards social institutions divorced from religious references.[38] This is not the place to address or even summarize the secularization debate, but we can point at some of its psychological underpinnings. Recently, Jürgen Habermas argued that modern societies, particularly in Europe and America, were in a "post-secular" stage.[39] This means that there is no doubt in most citizens' minds that a civilized and free society requires secular institutions. This consensus extends to the membership of most religious groups, which was not the case until the mid-twentieth century, as religious institutions were frequently trying to disrupt democratic institutions and gain political influence by siding with authoritarian regimes. In a post-secular age, according to Habermas, it is clear even to religious believers that religious activity is best protected by entirely secular institutions. The problem, however, is that this accommodation of secular democracy requires a painful "learning process".[40] But that process has not even begun, as far as some religious groups (e. g. Muslim extremists in Europe, Christian fundamentalists in the United States) are concerned.

Perhaps the secularization debates unduly confound two processes. Habermas points out that the survival of what he calls "pre-modern modes of thought" begs for explanation. Indeed, it would be difficult to understand it without mentioning two crucial domains of out evolved psychology, namely our psychology of cooperation and coalitions (see chapter 3) combined with the cultural fitness of superhuman agency beliefs (see chapter 2). On the one hand, we may be fairly certain that religious thought and behavior (super-human agency and associated rituals) are here to stay, as they constitute highly attention-grabbing and compelling phenomena. They are not usually defeated in their encounter with vastly more successful scientific and technical knowledge, as the latter requires much more effort. On the other hand, it is quite clear that in a free society people will certainly set up coalitional

---

36 See ORDESHOOK, *Game Theory and Political Theory* [1986].
37 See SEARS/HUDDY/JERVIS, *Oxford Handbook of Political Psychology* [2003].
38 WEBER, *Wirtschaft und Gesellschaft* [1956], 406.
39 See HABERMAS, *Zwischen Naturalismus und Religion* [2005].
40 HABERMAS, *Zwischen Naturalismus und Religion* [2005], 10.

identities and behaviors based on such highly efficient signals as religious statements. That the influence of such coalitions must be curbed for civil society to survive as a livable place is quite obvious, but that is intrinsically a political process, which can be achieved by motivated agents – it is not a matter of historical inevitability.

One might call these the cognitive and political secularization processes, respectively. These are not as intimately connected as classical secularization debates would suggest. "Historically religious thought and behavior in nation states has been dominated by quasi-monopolies, but the decline of such politically dominant institutions leaves lots of free space for non-institutional forms of religiosity. The resultant political situations do not vary along a single dimension of "more secular" to "less secular" but represent a more complex space. For instance, sociologists of religion have often commented on the contrast between Europe and the U.S. – but we cannot understand the difference simply in terms of less or more "religion". In the United States, there exists a highly efficient market of religious provision by competing guild-like institutions. As in many other domains of the economy, there is also a massive concentration of market power in the fold of a few very large corporate entities. Non-standard religious thoughts and practices, the usual competition of religious guilds, are relegated to obscure marginal groups. The European situation differs, not so much by the absence of religious thinking (notably of the informal kind, provided by mediums, shamans and the like) as by a widespread opposition to the encroachment of religious institutions into politics. To emphasize the multi-dimensional nature of these comparisons, consider China, not usually mentioned in such contexts although it may be relevant to see how a fifth of the world population handles these issues. There religious institutions do exist but cannot hope for much political influence – and never had much for millennia. Although most people are resolutely indifferent to metaphysical claims, the informal sector (which includes not just person-based provision, hut also traditional, ancestor-based cults) is striving. There are many roads to an accommodation of "religion" and civil society, but "secularization" may not be the best way to understand, or indeed to facilitate them.

Epilogue – fracture of an illusion

To many people, the scientific approach to religious thought and behavior, inspired by what I called the Kant-Darwin axis, is a disappointing enterprise. The starting point is inspiring enough – a proper, naturalistic understanding of a set of concepts and norms that seem highly recurrent in human minds and terribly important to some of them. People then grudgingly concede the need to go through meticulous definitions and descriptions of experimental paradigms. In the end, however, the results seem invariably frustrating.

Anyone who works in this field has had to respond to exasperated questions from readers and listeners, to the effect that this budding science does not even mention the questions they wanted addressed: Is religion nothing but mental activity? Does it undermine civil society? Is it a natural feature of human minds? Scientific approaches seem to skirt these issues and replace simple answers with never-ending redefinitions and qualifications. Paraphrasing Karl Kraus's sardonic comment, we could say that scholars of religions and their audience are in complete harmony, as the latter do not hear what the former say and the former do not want to say what the latter expect.[41]

It is an inconvenient fact, perhaps, that the scientific explanation of religious matters really does not need the notion of "religion", any more than the study of chemistry has need for the notion of "fire" or biology for "trees". It took many a decade, in some cases centuries, for scientific reasoning to get rid of some of these terms, so apparently obvious and precise in their reference, yet ultimately misleading. So it may take a while before scientific studies of religious phenomena develop the right tools and provide us with sufficient, explanatory, predictive models of religious psychology and social dynamics. My prediction is that such models will roughly follow the kind of explanatory agenda I described at the beginning of this essay as the Kant-Darwin axis, the notion that religious phenomena are explained by the way minds work, and the way minds work is a consequence of our evolved nature. These two assumptions were also the starting point for Sigmund Freud's main treatise on religion, which inspired the title, if little else, of this essay. Freud was resolutely optimistic about the evolutionary, neurally-based science of religion, and cautious about people's desire to find more than can be found in science:

No, our science is not an illusion. But it would be an illusion to expect that we can get elsewhere, what science cannot give us."[42]

This leads us back to the question, why we should be so concerned with the proper understanding of religious phenomena, and does it really matter that "religion" is mostly an illusory object, the construct of some religious institutions, with no real reference in human psychology or social dynamics? It does matter – I tried to suggest here that this not a purely academic debate. People who think that there is such a thing as "religion" and construe is as the sleep of reason, will certainly not achieve their goal of extirpating religious thoughts from human minds, as they are attacking windmills. Conversely, and certainly more importantly, others deplore that free societies are so clearly detached from "religion" and see the latter as obviously superior to the constraints of civilized existence, so that it makes perfect sense to coerce

41 KRAUS, *Sprüche und Widersprüche* [1955], 165.
42 FREUD: „Nein, unsere Wissenschaft ist keine Illusion. Eine Illusion aber wäre es zu glauben, daß wir anderswoher bekommen könnten, was sie uns nicht geben kann." *Die Zukunft einer Illusion* [1928], 116.

human beings into the proper religious existence. We must resist those people, since all theocratic societies are versions of Hell on earth. But that is all that more difficult if we share some of their delusions, notably about the existence of a special domain of thought and action that is "religion".

Afterword

In this book, Pascal Boyer makes a significant contribution to understanding religious thought and behavior by taking the perspective of evolutionary cognitive science. This book gives ample evidence of Boyer's productivity during his tenure as Fellow at the Goethe University in Frankfurt. We were grateful to be his conversation partners, even though we belong to the "guild" of theologians, who according to Boyer, are superfluous or even harmful to the religious impulse.

We want to comment in this short afterward on two major lines of thought in Boyer's essay from the perspective of Christian theology. The first concerns his overarching research strategy, the second his understanding of religion.

Boyer sees himself as pursuing an approach marked by the Enlightenment and secular reason, on the one hand, and the tradition of Darwinian evolutionary thinking, on the other. Though he describes himself as an atheist, he is a very pacific one in comparison to the kind of militant atheist missionary spirit of those like Richard Dawkins. This does not mean that he is always polite and tolerant to religion; he employs drastic vocabulary to challenge the very concept of "religion" from his evolutionary standpoint and considers religious behavior "parasitic" on cognitive faculties of the evolved mind. For American religious institutions, for instance, he argues that tax exemptions can not be justified on the basis of a misguided notion of religion.

Boyer's ingenious idea is to combine the traditions of Enlightenment and evolution to understand the religious impulse. This is the Kant-Darwin axis. Using the tools of modern evolutionary cognitive neuroscience, religion can become the object of scientific investigation rather than the province of folk psychology. That is Boyer's scientific approach to understanding religions.

Can this understanding of religion be helpful for Christian theology? Why is this explanation of religion interesting for theology at all? There are several reasons: First, the question of whether the human person is *capax dei* has always been an issue within theology viz. what are the epistemological preconditions for understanding the proclamation of the Gospel? That is, how can theological insights become intelligible to the human mind? For twentieth-century Protestant theology, this is the problem of the so called "point of contact" or *Anknüpfungspunkt* between the human and divine.

Secondly, ever since the modern shift in theology initiated by Schleiermacher leading to the studying religious consciousness in various stages of its development – culminating in Christ's "Kräftigkeit des Gottesbewusstseins" – the religious mind has been a focus of theological understanding. It is therefore not surprising that in the nineteenth century the "history of religions school" or *Religionsgeschichtliche Schule* emerged as a sub-branch within the context of the growing movement of German historicism. Hence even prior to William James' *Varieties of Religious Experience*, Protestantism was aware of the diversity of religious experience. Finally, in our time the necessity of religious dialog, often initiated by Christians who follow this experiential tradition, it is imperative to understand how the religious mind works.

Given these diverse *Weltanschauungen*, what can be said about Boyer's research strategy in the context of secular reason, and its implied challenge to religious truth claims? What can be said about the secular research strategy pursued along Boyer's Kant-Darwin axis and about the limitations of human reason from the standpoint of Protestant theology? Is it a danger, an intellectual challenge, or is it a relatively harmless and misguided attempt to understand religion?

Let us consider one strain of this tradition Boyer cites not fully appreciated by secular scientists themselves. To put it very briefly, Darwin is in a certain sense the apex of Christian missionary strategy, dating back to the founding of the Royal Society in 1660. Theologians were among the founding fathers of the Royal Society and they argued that knowledge of God the creator was fostered by knowledge of the creation and that natural science could contribute to a natural knowledge of God. Bishop John Wilkins in particular made this Christian missionary research strategy explicit in his book "Of The Principles And Duties Of Natural Religion", first published in 1675. As it turned out, this missionary strategy developed into a scientific research program. In nearly all fields of the emerging scientific revolution of the seventeenth-century, this missionary goal was represented by key figures. This is well-known in the case physics with Isaac Newton. But it was also true in the botany of John Ray. The same holds true in medicine and anatomy. Lorenz Heister's classic textbook in anatomy, which was widely-used across Europe in the eighteenth century and was used as a manual for the students of medicine, gives witness to the productive role of natural theology in medicine. This Natural theology culminated in the famous work of William Paley: *Natural Theology or Evidence of the Existence and Attributes of the Deity, collected from the appearances of nature.* Thus natural theology paved the way for natural science and contributed significantly to the emergence of evolutionary thinking. Even the key notions of *adaptation* and *fitness* were coined by natural theology and elaborated by William Paley. Without the pioneering work of these sincere pious scientists and theologians, Darwin's great intellectual breakthrough would have been inconceivable. His genius was to break through the mental barrier created by the theological framework. This was an intellectual, scientific and existential risk Darwin was willing to take. By reframing the theological context of adaptation and fitness – as being an evidence of an intelligent creator – to the testable scientific hypothesis of variation/mutation and natural selection he demolished the whole program of natural theology. God as a wise intelligent designer became superfluous and could be substituted by these natural principles. Darwin made the traditional view of man as the image of God (and the corresponding thesis of monogenesis) intellectually vacuous. However, it was only an *imago* and not God himself which was at stake. Darwin could have asked about the speculative limitations of our reason as Kant did as early as 1786 with the publication of his *Critique of Pure Reason* by dismantling Physico-Theology and its proofs of God's existence – Darwin might have asked whether religion itself could be interpreted as an evolutionary process, as it was suggested to him in 1869 by the German zoologist Gustav Jäger in his book "Die Darwin'sche Theorie und ihre Stellung zu Moral und Religion". But he took another route. Although he was originally a theologian of the decidedly Paleyian stripe, Darwin finally became atheist. Was this personal development dictated by the findings of his theory? Today, some theologians argue that the theory of evolution does not of necessity lead to atheism as adherents of a modern atheist world view claim. Rather, evolution is open to a theological interpretation, along the lines of the traditional *creatio continua*, advocated originally by Luther, and more recently and convincingly by the *process theology* inspired by Alfred N. Whitehead. Hence, according to these figures, evolutionary thinking along Darwinian lines is both open to theological as well as atheistic interpretation. This is a matter of competing *Weltanschauungen*, and not a conclusion dictated by science itself.

What about the Kantian line of the axis? If one takes seriously, that the "God-talk" characteristic of the British program of natural theology which was consistent with a Kantian image, model or metaphor of God then, of course the whole program of natural theology might be reconsidered in the framework of epistemology. This is exactly what Kant did when he demolished the tradition of German *Physicotheologie*, the German equivalent of British natural theology. After Kant's attack, this way of reasoning disappeared from German theology and it is the reason why German Protestant theology believed that it was not essentially threatened by nineteenth-century Darwinian evolution. The secularization of reason in Protestant theology took place much earlier in Germany than it did on the British Isles. In fact, one can argue and this is one prominent line of interpretation, that Kant's secularization of reason is itself the culmination of Lutheran theology. Kant was raised in religious context of introspective German pietism so that this emphasis on religious affections is perhaps the precursor to his critical, Copernican revolution in philosophy Hence, not only Pietism, but Luther himself paved the way to the modern secularization of reason. By breaking down the Neo-thomistic synthesis of faith and reason, Luther and the other Protestant reformers set reason free to operate in a secular context without being distorted by theological interventions. Reason, according to Luther and Kant, must humbly recognize its limitations and acknowledge God, but it is equally God's greatest gift to humankind to explore the world by engaging in science.

Thus one can argue that modern secular rationality has its roots in theological reasoning. In the case of secular evolutionary thinking, we need to recognize its origin in British natural theology. In the case of epistemology, especially in Germany, we need to recognize the role of pietism and the contribution of Lutheran theology to the development of secular reason.

But Boyer's major claim is that there is such a thing as religion. What he means by "religion" is basically folk religion, since it is this common sense religious thoughts and behaviors which are determined by the brain. Subsequent theological reflection is rather the work of economically rational and self-interested religious-guilds, operating in conjunction with the powers of statecraft.

Based on sound experimental data and findings in neuroscience, Boyer wants to show that certain properties of religion emerged independently of each other as the result of a very specific selective evolutionary pressure. These properties are not necessarily linked together. Thus – and that is his slightly ironic claim – religious phenomena are parasitic on basically non-religious activity of the brain; this is a purely functional interpretation of religion, meaning that the content, i. e. the essence of religious belief, is unimportant. However, there indications based on empirical data, that at least in some areas religious content does play a key identity-forming role. For example, Richard Sosis has shown in his famous research that the longevity of nineteenth-century American communes is results in part from their religious commit-ments. And very recently, Michael Blume has collected data from a Swiss census that substantiates the thesis that reproduction rates are positively correlated with religious affiliation. But perhaps Boyer would argue that these studies have to do with what we call the "higher religions", and are not in the focus of his research.

In describing religion, Boyer identifies the following aspects which can be traced to evolved faculties of the brain: mental representations of non-physical agents (e. g., ghosts, ancestors, spirits etc.), artefacts associated with these agents, rituals to interact with non-physical agents, moral intuitions, experiences that bring about contact with non-physical agents, and the ethnic specification of religion. Boyer tries to identify the underlying evolutionary mechanisms in the brain which are advantageous in this evolutionary game. Evolutionary mechanisms are essential to this process and specific religious claims are understood as their by-products. From this standpoint, ritual behavior is significant because it can be functionally interpreted as danger protection and attention grabbing device. Echoing Freud, Boyer notes that rituals and rites resemble obsessive-compulsive disorders (OCD in their rigidity and redundancy). One could ask, however, if this approach to religious phenomena explains the strong association between rites and myth often found in indigenous religions. Interestingly, mythology is missing from the list of Boyer's universal traits of religious thought and behavior. And what is about rites or rituals that rely on historical facts and are therefore used for commemoration rather than attention-grabbing? For instance, agricultural rites in the Old Testament were reinterpreted as festivals to commemorate the Exodus of the Jews from Egypt. Moreover, the rites of Christianity such as the Eucharist claim to have a historical foundation.

Do these findings and claims have any relevance for Christian theology in general and Protestant theology in particular? As stated above, Protestantism since Luther and Calvin has been suspicious of human religiosity. In particular, Calvin objected to the way the human mind produces religion (*mens humana perpetua fabrica idolatrorum*). Seen from this broad perspective, Boyer's research is very much in tune with this iconoclastic element in Protestant theology. Indeed, it supplements this approach by being able to explain, as these theologians were not, why this kind of religiosity seems to be so persistent. It appears that these features of religiosity have a specific inertia as a result of evolution which makes them partly immune to the contents of beliefs spread by the self-interested guilds of theologians.

Boyer's understanding of religion as parasitic upon evolutionary developments poses a certain problem. Why does religious reflection exist at all? Can its existence be explained from the perspective of evolutionary cognitive science? Basically two elements of the theology of world religions are at stake in this issue. The first is the understanding of salvation, the second is divine transcendence. As a protest against domestication of transcendence, Old Testament prophets fought their battle against many aspects of what Boyer describes as the features of religion stemming from the evolutionary tools of the brain. The problem here is to identify the frontier between real transcendence and human religiousness, whether as a by-product or no. This could be studied in detail in further research by comparison between features of the religious mind and their prophetic rejection in the Old Testament. Although this short summary is inadequate to describe the riches to be found in this book, Boyer has certainly opened up a new field of further investigation into the phenomenon of religion. With his work a further chapter in discussion of the entire project of naturalization of religion has been opened.

Elisabeth Gräb-Schmidt
Wolfgang Achtner

Bibliography

ABED, R.T./DE PAUW, K.W., An evolutionary hypothesis for obsessive compulsive disorder: a psychological immune system? Behavioural Neurology 11(4), 1998, 245–250.

AINSLIE, G., Précis of breakdown of will, Behavioral and Brain Sciences 28(5), 2005, 635–673.

ARGYLE, M., The psychological explanation of religious experience, Psyke & Logos 11(2), 1990, 267–274.

ATRAN, S.A., In Gods We Trust: The Evolutionary Landscape of Religion, Oxford 2002.

AZARI, N.P. et al., Neural correlates of religious experience, European Journal of Neuroscience 13(8), 2001, 1649–1652.

BARRETT, H.C., Cognitive development and the understanding of animal behavior, in: B.J. ELLIS (Ed.), Origins of the Social Mind: Evolutionary Psychology and Child Development, New York 2005, xv, 540, 438–467.

BARRETT, J.L., Anthropomorphism, Intentional Agents, and Conceptualizing God, unpublished PhD dissertation, Cornell University 1996.

BARRETT, J.L., Cognitive constraints on Hindu concepts of the divine, Journal for the Scientific Study of Religion 37, 1998, 608–619.

BARRETT, J.L., Why Would Anyone Believe in God? Walnut Creek, CA 2004.

BARRETT, J.L./KEIL, F.C., Conceptualizing a nonnatural entity: Anthropomorphism in God concepts, Cognitive Psychology 31(3), 1996, 219–247.

BARRETT, J.L./NYHOF, M., Spreading non-natural concepts: The role of intuitive conceptual structures in memory and transmission of cultural materials, Journal of Cognition and Culture 1, 2001, 69–100.

BELL, C.M., Ritual Theory, Ritual Practice, New York 1992.

BENTLEY, R., The Folly of Atheism, and (What is Now Called) Deism, Even with Respect to the Present Life: A Sermon Preached in the Church of St. Martin in the Fields, March the VII, 1691/2: Being the First of the Lecture Founded by the Honourable Robert Boyle, Esquire, London 1692.

BLOCH, M., Symbols, song, dance, and features of articulation: Is religion an extreme form of traditional authority? European Journal of Sociology 15, 1974, 55–81.

BOYATZIS, C.J., A critique of models of religious experience, The International Journal for the Psychology of Religion 11(4), 2001, 247–258.

BOYD, R./RICHERSON, P.J., Solving the puzzle of human cooperation, in: S.C. LEVINSON/P. JAISSON (Eds.), Evolution and Culture, Cambridge, MA 2006, 105–132.

BOYER, P., Tradition as Truth and Communication: A Cognitive Description of Traditional Discourse, Cambridge 1990.

BOYER, P., The Naturalness of Religious Ideas: A Cognitive Theory of Religion, Berkeley, CA 1994.

BOYER, P., *Functional origins* of religious concepts: conceptual and strategic selection in evolved minds [Malinowski Lecture 1999], Journal of the Royal Anthropological Institute 6, 2000, 195–214.

BOYER, P., *Natural epistemology* or evolved metaphysics? Developmental evidence for early-developed, intuitive, category-specific, incomplete, and stubborn metaphysical presumptions, Philosophical Psychology 13(3), 2000, 277–297.

BOYER, P., Religion Explained. Evolutionary Origins of Religious Thought, New York 2001.

BOYER, P./BEDOIN, N./HONORE, S., Relative contributions from kind- and domain-concepts to inferences concerning unfamiliar exemplars: developmental change and domain differences, Cognitive Development 15, 2001, 345–362.

BOYER, P./LIENARD, P., Why ritualized behavior in humans? Precaution systems and action-parsing in developmental, pathological and cultural rituals, Behavioral & Brain Sciences 29, 2006, 1–56.

BOYER, P./RAMBLE, C., Cognitive templates for religious concepts: cross-cultural evidence for recall of counter-intuitive representations, Cognitive Science 25, 2001, 535–564.

BROWN, D.E., Human Universals, New York 1991.

BULBULIA, J., Religious costs as adaptations that signal altruistic intention, Evolution and Cognition 10(1), 2004, 19–42.

BURKHARDT, M.A./NAGAI-JACOBSON, M.G., Spirituality: Living Our Connectedness, Albany 2001.

BUSS, D.M./HASELTON, M.G./SHACKELFORD, T.K./BLESKE, A.L./WAKEFIELD, J.C., Adaptations, exaptations, and spandrels, Am Psychol 53(5), 1998, 533–548.

COSMIDES, L./TOOBY, J., Consider the source: The evolution of adaptations for decoupling and metarepresentation, in: D. SPERBER (Ed.), Metarepresentations: A Multidisciplinary Perspective, New York 2000, 53–115.

COSMIDES, L./TOOBY, J. (Eds.), Neurocognitive Adaptations Designed for Social Exchange, Hoboken, NJ 2005.

COWARD, H.G./LIPNER, J./YOUNG, K.K., Hindu Ethics: Purity, Abortion, and Euthanasia, Albany 1989.

CRONK, L., Evolutionary theories of morality and the manipulative use of signals, Zygon 29(1), 1994, 81.

DAVIS, C.F., The Evidential Force of Religious Experience, Oxford, UK/New York 1989.

DAWKINS, R., The God Delusion, Boston 2006.

DE ALBUQUERQUE, C.L./PAES-MACHADO, E., The hazing machine: the shaping of Brazilian military police recruits, Policing & Society 14(2), 2004, 175–192.

DELSUC, F./CATZEFLIS, F.M./STANHOPE, M.J./DOUZERY, E.J., The evolution of armadillos, anteaters and sloths depicted by nuclear and mitochondrial phylogenies: implications for the status of the enigmatic fossil Eurotamandua, Proc Biol Sci 268(1476), 2001, 1605–1615.

DORIS, J.M./KNOBE, J./WOOLFOLK, R.L., Variantism about responsibility, Nous-Supplement: Philosophical Perspectives 21, 2007, 183–214.

DOUGLAS, M., Purity and Danger: An Analysis of Concepts of Pollution and Taboo, New York 1966.

DOUGLAS, M., Natural symbols: Explorations in Cosmology (Pantheon paperbacks ed.), New York 1982.

DULANEY, S./FISKE, A.P., Cultural rituals and obsessive-compulsive disorder: Is there a common psychological mechanism? Ethos 22(3), 1994, 243–283.

ELSTER, J., Ulysses and the Sirens: Studies in Rationality and Irrationality, Cambridge, UK/New York 1979.

FIDDICK, L., Domains of deontic reasoning: Resolving the discrepancy between the cognitive and moral reasoning literatures, Quarterly Journal of Experimental Psychology: Human Experimental Psychology 57 A(3), 2004, 447–474.

FIELDING, H., The History of Tom Jones a Foundling, London 1749.

FOOT, P., Killing, letting die, and euthanasia: a reply to holly Smith Goldman, Analysis 41, 1981, 159–160.

FRANK, R.H., Passions within Reason. The Strategic Role of the Emotions, New York 1988.

FRANK, R.H., Cooperation through emotional commitment, in: R.M. NESSE (Ed.), Evolution and the Capacity for Commitment, New York 2001, 57–76.

FREUD, S., Die Zukunft einer Illusion, Leipzig ²1928.

FREUD, S., Zwangsbehandlungen und Religionsübungen, in: FREUD (Ed.), Gesammelte Werke von Sigmund Freud, chronologisch geordnet, Vol. 7, London 1948[1906], 107–116.

GELLNER, E., Relativism and the Social Sciences, Cambridge Cambridgeshire/New York 1985.

GINTIS, H., Strong reciprocity and human sociality, Journal of Theoretical Biology 206(2), 2000, 169–179.

GOETHE, J. W. v., Faust. Ein Fragment, ächte Ausgabe, erster Druck, zweite Form, Leipzig 1790.

GOODY, J., Literacy in Traditional Societies, Cambridge 1968.

GOODY, J., The Domestication of the Savage Mind, Cambridge 1977.

GOODY, J., The Logic of Writing and the Organization of Society, Cambridge 1986.

GOULD, S.J., Nonoverlapping Magisteria: science and religion are not in conflict, for their teachings occupy distinctly different domains, Natural History 106(2), 1997, 16–22.

GREEN, L./MYERSON, J., A discounting framework for choice with delayed and probabilistic rewards, Psychological Bulletin 130(5), 2004, 769–792.

GREENE, J., Cognitive neuroscience and the structure of the moral mind, in: P. CARRUTHERS (Ed.), The Innate Mind: Structure and Contents, New York 2005, 338–352.

GUTHRIE, R.D., The Nature of Paleolithic Art, Chicago 2005.

GUTHRIE, S.E., Faces in the Clouds: A New Theory of Religion, New York 1993.

HABERMAS, J., Zwischen Naturalismus und Religion, Frankfurt am Main 2005.

HAIDT, J., The new synthesis in moral psychology, Science 316 (5827), 2007, 998–1002.

HAMILTON, W.D., The general evolution of social behavior (I and II), Journal of Theoretical Biology 7, 1964, 1–52.

HITCHENS, C., God is Not Great: How Religion Poisons Everything, New York 2007.

HOUSE OF COMMONS, Criminal Justice and Public Order Act 1994, Chapter 33.

HUME, D., Natural History of Religion, London 1757.

HUME, D., A Treatise of Human Nature: Being an Attempt to Introduce the Experimental Method of Reasoning into Moral Subjects, London 1739

HUME, D., Dialogues Concerning Natural Religion, London ²1779.

HUMPHREY, C./LAIDLAW, J., Archetypal Actions: A Theory of Ritual as a Mode of Action and the Case of the Jain Puja, Oxford 1993.

IRONS, W., Religion as a hard-to-fake sign of commitment, in: R. NESSE (Ed.), Evolution and the Capacity for Commitment, New York 2002, 292–309.

JACK, A.I./ROBBINS, P., The illusory triumph of machine over mind: Wegner's eliminativism and the real promise of psychology, Behavioral & Brain Sciences 27(5), 2004, 665–666.

JAMES, W., The Varieties of Religious Experience: A Study in Human Nature Being the Gifford Lectures on Natural Religion Delivered at Edinburgh in 1901–1902, New York 1902.

KANT, I., Critik der reinen Vernunft, Riga 1781.

KANWISHER, N., Domain specificity in face perception, Nature Neuroscience 3(8), 2000, 759–763.

KIERKEGAARD, S., Either/Or: A Fragment of Life, abridged, translated and with an introduction by A. Hannay, London/New York 1992.

KRAUS, K., Sprüche und Widersprüche, Wien: Die Fackel 1909, 15. Februar, Nr. 273, 40–48.

KRAUS, K., Sprüche und Widersprüche, in: K. Kraus, Beim Wort Genommen. München 1955, 11–178.

LAWRENCE, B.B., Defenders of God: The Fundamentalist Revolt against the Modern Age, San Francisco 1989.

LAWSON, E.T./McCAULEY, R.N., Rethinking Religion: Connecting Cognition and Culture, Cambridge 1990.

LESLIE, A.M./FRIEDMAN, O./GERMAN, T.P., Core mechanisms in 'theory of mind', Trends in Cognitive Sciences 8(12), 2004, 529–533.

LESSER, E., The New American Spirituality: A Seeker's Guide, New York 1999.

LEWIS, C.S., Mere Christianity, New York 1997.

LIENARD, P./BOYER, P., Whence Collective Rituals? A Cultural Selection Model of Ritualized Behavior, American Anthropologist 108(4), 2006, 814–827.

LOEWENSTEIN, G./READ, D. (Eds.), Time and Decision: Economic and Psychological Perspectives on Intertemporal Choice, New York 2003.

MALLE, B.F./MOSES, L.J./BALDWIN, D.A. (Eds.), Intentions and Intentionality: Foundations of Social Cognition, Cambridge, MA 2001.

MARTY, M.E./APPLEBY, R.S. (Eds.), Fundamentalisms observed, Chicago 1991.

MARTY, M.E./APPLEBY, R.S. (Eds.), *Fundamentalism and Society:* Reclaiming the Sciences, the Family and Education, Chicago 1993.

MARTY, M.E./APPLEBY, R.S. (Eds.), *Fundamentalism and the State:* Remaking Polities, Economies and Militancy, Chicago 1993.

MARTY, M.E./APPLEBY, R.S. (Eds.), Accounting for Fundamentalisms: The Dynamic Character of Movements, Chicago 1994.

MATTHEWS, S., Personal identity, multiple personality disorder, and moral personhood, Philosophical Psychology 11(1), 1998, 67–88.

MCCAULEY, R.N., The naturalness of religion and the unnaturalness of science, in: F. KEIL/R. WILSON (Eds.), Explanation and Cognition, Cambridge, MA 2000, 61–85.

MCCUTCHEON, R.T., Manufacturing Religion: The Discourse on Sui Generis Religion and the Politics of Nostalgia, New York 1997.

MCMULLIN, N., The encyclopedia of religion: a critique from the perspective of the history of the Japanese religious traditions, Method & Theory in the Study of Religion 1, 1989, 80–96.

MITHEN, S.J., The Prehistory of the Mind, London 1996.

MOEHLE, D., Cognitive dimensions of religious experiences, Journal of Experimental Social Psychology 19(2), 1983, 122–145.

MUSALLAM, B., Sex and Society in Islam: Birth control Before the Nineteenth Century, Cambridge/New York 1983.

NEEDHAM, R., Polythetic classification: convergence and consequences, Man 10, 1975, 349–369.

NEWBERG, A.B./D'AQUILI, E.G., The neuropsychology of spiritual experience, in: H.G. KOENIG et al. (Eds.), Handbook of Religion and Mental Health, San Diego 1998, 75–94.

ORDESHOOK, P.C., Game Theory and Political Theory: An Introduction, New York 1986.

OTTO, R., Das Heilige, Breslau [4]1920.

PERSINGER, M.A., Near-death experiences and ecstasy: A product of the organization of the human brain, in: S.D. SALA et al. (Eds.), Mind Myths: Exploring Popular Assumptions about the Mind and Brain, Chichester 1999, 85–99.

POSNER, R.A., A Theory of primitive society, with special reference to law, in: F. PARISI (Ed.), The Collected Essays of Richard A. Posner, Volume 2: The Economics of Private Law, Northampton 2001, 3–55.

PREUS, J.S., Explaining religion: criticism and theory from Bodin to Freud, Religion 19, 1989, 324–329.

PRICE, M.E./COSMIDES, L./TOOBY, J., Punitive sentiment as an anti-free rider psychological device, Evolution & Human Behavior 23(3), 2002, 203–231.

PROUDFOOT, W., Religious Experience, Berkeley 1985.

PYYSIÄINEN, I., How Religion Works: Towards a New Cognitive Science of Religion, Leiden 2001.

PYYSIÄINEN, I., Magic, Miracles, And Religion: A Scientist's Perspective, Walnut Creek, CA 2004.

RAICHLE, M.E., Modern phrenology: maps of human cortical function, Annals of the
    New York Academy of Sciences 882, 1999, 107.

RAPOPORT, J.L./FISKE, A., The new biology of obsessive-compulsive disorder:
    implications for evolutionary psychology, Perspectives in Biology and Medicine
    41(2), 1998, 159–175.

RATCLIFFE, M., Neurotheology: A science of what? In: P. McNAMARA (Ed.), Where
    God and Science Meet: How Brain and Evolutionary Studies Alter Our Under-
    standing of Religion, Volume 2: The Neurology of Religious Experience, Westport
    2006, 81–104.

REINHART, A.K., Before Revelation: the Boundaries of Muslim Moral Thought,
    Albany, N.Y 1995.

RIDLEY, M., The Origins of Virtue: Human Instincts and the Evolution of
    Cooperation, New York 1996.

ROUSSEAU, J.-J., Émile, ou De l'Éducation, Amsterdam 1762.

ROZIN, P./MILLMAN, L./NEMEROFF, Operation of the laws of sympathetic magic in
    disgust and other domains, Journal of Personality and Social Psychology 50(4),
    1986, 703–712.

SAARNI, C., Cognition, context, and goals: Significant components in social-
    emotional effectiveness, Social Development 10(1), 2001, 125–129.

SALER, B., Conceptualizing Religion: Immanent Anthropologists, Transcendent
    Natives and Unbounded Categories, Leiden 1993.

SCHELLING, T., The Strategy of Conflict, Cambridge, MA 1960.

SCHLEIERMACHER, F., Über die Religion: Reden an die Gebildeten unter ihren
    Verächtern, Berlin 1799.

SCHNUR, S., Fraternity Hazing: A Multi-Perspective Analysis of a Universal
    Phenomenon, ProQuest Information & Learning, US 2008.

SCOTT, G.E., Moral Personhood: An Essay in the Philosophy of Moral Psychology,
    Albany 1990.

SEARS, D.O./HUDDY, L./JERVIS, R., Oxford Handbook of Political Psychology, New
    York 2003.

SHARF, R.H., Experience, in: M.C. TAYLOR (Ed.), Critical Terms for Religious Studies,
    Chicago 1998, 94–116.

SMITH, A., The Theory of Moral Sentiments: To Which is Added a Dissertation on the
    Origin of Languages, London ³1767.

SMITH, J.Z., Imagining Religion: From Babylon to Jonestown, Chicago 1982.

SMITH, V.L., Constructivist and ecological rationality in economics, American
    Economic Review 93(3), 2003, 465–508.

SØRENSEN, J., 'The morphology and function of magic' revisited, in: V. ANTTONEN/I.
    PYYSIAINEN (Eds.), Current Approaches in the Cognitive Study of Religion,
    London 2002, 35–43.

SOSIS, R., Religion and intragroup cooperation: Preliminary results of a comparative
    analysis of utopian communities, Cross-Cultural Research: The Journal of
    Comparative Social Science 34(1), 2000, 70–87.

SOSIS, R., Why aren't we all hutterites? Costly signaling theory and religious behavior, Human Nature 14(2), 2003, 91 – 127.

SOSIS, R./BRESSLER, E.R., Cooperation and commune longevity: A test of the costly signaling theory of religion, Cross-Cultural Research: The Journal of Comparative Social Science 37(2), 2003, 211 – 239.

SPERBER, D., Intuitive and reflective beliefs, Mind & Language 12(1), 1997, 67 – 83.

STAAL, F., Rules without Meaning: Ritual, Mantras, and the Human Sciences, New York 1990.

STICH, S., From Folk-psychology to Cognitive Science: The Case against Belief, Cambridge, MA 1983.

SUPREME COURT OF THE UNITED STATES, United States v. Ballard, U.S. 78, 1944, 322.

SUPREME COURT OF THE UNITED STATES, Thomas v. Seeger, U.S. 163, 1965, 380.

SUPREME COURT OF THE UNITED STATES, Thomas v. Review Board, U.S. 707, 1981, 450.

SZECHTMAN, H./WOODY, E., Obsessive-compulsive disorder as a disturbance of security motivation, Psychological Review 111(1), 2004, 111 – 127.

TAYLOR, M., Imaginary Companions and the Children Who Create Them, New York 1999.

TAYLOR, M./CARLSON, S.M., The relation between individual differences in fantasy and theory of mind, Child Development 68(3), 1997, 436 – 455.

TEASDALE, W., The Mystic Heart: Discovering a Universal Spirituality in the World's Religions, Novato 1999.

THOMSON, J. J., A defense of abortion, Philosophy & Public Affairs 1, 1971, 47 – 66.

TOOBY, J./DEVORE, I., The reconstruction of hominid behavioral evolution through strategic modeling, in: W. Kinzey (Ed.), The Evolution of Human Behaviour: Primate Models, New York 1987, 183 – 237.

TRIVERS, R.L., The evolution of reciprocal altruism, Quarterly Review of Biology 46, 1971, 35 – 57.

TURIEL, E., The Development of Social Knowledge: Morality and Convention, Cambridge 1983.

VOLTAIRE, F. M. A. D., Dictionnaire philosophique, portatif, Paris 1764.

WAAIJMAN, K., Spirituality: Forms, Foundations, Methods, Leuven/Dudley, MA 2002.

WEBER, M., Wirtschaft und Gesellschaft: Grundriss der Verstehenden Soziologie, Tübingen ⁴1956.

WHEATCROFT, D.J./PRICE, T.D., Reciprocal cooperation in avian mobbing: playing nice pays, Trends in Ecology & Evolution 23(8), 2008, 416 – 419.

WHITEN, A. (Ed.), Natural Theories of Mind: The Evolution, Development and Simulation of Everyday Mind-Reading, Oxford 1991.

WIEBE, D., The Politics of Religious Studies: the Continuing Conflict with Theology in the Academy, New York 1998.

WILLIAMS, G.C., Adaptation and Natural Selection: A Critique of Some Current Evolutionary Thought, Princeton 1966.

WOLPERT, L., The Unnatural Nature of Science, London 1992.

ZAHAVI, A./ZAHAVI, A., The Handicap Principle: a Missing Piece of Darwin's Puzzle, New York 1997.

ZOHAR, A.H./FELZ, L., Ritualistic behavior in young children, J Abnorm Child Psychol 29(2), 2001, 121–128.

ZUNSHINE, L., Why We Read Fiction: Theory of Mind and the Novel, Columbus 2006.